CONNECTING ACROSS CULTURES AND CONTINENTS

Black Women
Speak Out on
Identity, Race and Development

Edited by Achola O. Pala

UNIFEM

United Nations Development Fund
for Women (UNIFEM)
New York, USA

The United Nations Development Fund for Women (UNIFEM) was created as a result of the energetic advocacy of women at the 1975 International Women's Year (IWY) Tribune in Mexico City. Established by the United Nations in 1976 as the Voluntary Fund for the UN Decade for Women, UNIFEM became an autonomous organization within the UN family in 1985. UNIFEM provides direct technical and financial support to programmes that promote women. By supporting the full participation of women in the developing world to achieve their objectives of sustainable economic and social development and equality, UNIFEM works to improve the quality of life for all. This collection of articles was published by UNIFEM's Advocacy Facility which prepares and disseminates state of the art information on women and development.

The views expressed in this book are those of the authors and do not necessarily represent the views of UNIFEM, the United Nations or any of its affiliated organizations.

Connecting Across Cultures and Continents: Black Women Speak Out on Identity, Race and Development
Edited by Achola O. Pala
ISBN 0-912917-35-0

© 1995 The United Nations Development Fund for Women

United Nations Development Fund for Women
304 East 45th Street, 6th Floor, New York, NY 10017 USA
Phone: (212) 906-6400 Fax: (212) 906-6705

All UNIFEM publications are distributed by Women, Ink.
777 UN Plaza, 3rd Floor, New York, NY 10017 USA
Phone: (212) 687-8633 Fax: (212) 661-2704

Many thanks to Terri L. Jewell, editor of *The Black Woman's Gumbo Ya-Ya. Quotations by Black Women,* and The Crossing Press, Freedom, California for compiling the words of Black women globally.

Cover & book design by a. piccolo graphics
Cover illustration adapted from poster designed by M. Quiroga

Table of Contents

Preface 1
Ana Maria Brasileiro

Introduction 3
Achola O. Pala

Chapter 1 Defining Black Feminism .11
Sueli Carneiro

Chapter 2 Black Women and Identity in the Caribbean:
Out of the Quagmire 19
Eintou Pearl Springer

Chapter 3 From Fractured Identities, a New Consciousness 31
Glenda Simms

Chapter 4 Apartheid and Identity: Black Women in South Africa . .39
Danisa E. Baloyi

Chapter 5 Power, Racism and Identity 47
Sergia Galvan

Chapter 6 Women in the Caribbean: The Quadruple Burden of
Gender, Race, Class and Imperialism 53
Peggy Antrobus

Chapter 7 Gender-responsive Agenda for Equitable Development . .61
Felicia Ekejiuba

Chapter 8 The Impact of the Black Consciousness
and Women's Movements on Black Women's
Identity: Intercontinental Empowerment 71
Andrée Nicola McLaughlin

Bibliography 85

The responsibility of the chronicler is to hear what people truly are saying about their experiences. To use their rhythm and cadence of expression to define and describe and not delete it from the retelling.

– Barbara Omolade

Acknowledgements

This book is a result of the presentations, discussions and contributions of Black women who attended and participated in two UNIFEM-funded panels on Black women's identities and livelihoods at the Fifth International Interdisciplinary Congress on Women held in Costa Rica in February 1993.

The book would not have been possible without the support of a number of people. First, many thanks go to the women who answered UNIFEM's call in 1993 and agreed to participate in the Congress. Although not all their papers are included in this volume, their ideas and their perspectives greatly enriched the deliberations of the two panels. We also want to thank Mirta Gonzalez and organizers of the Congress for their encouragement and support in the planning and presentation of these panels. We are grateful to Sandra Martin for managing the entire logistical arrangements which involved communication and follow-up between three continents.

We want to thank the moderators for the two panels: Dr. Filomina Chioma Steady for the panel on Black women's livelihoods and Professor Ruth Simms Hamilton for the panel on Black women's identities. Dr. Andrée McLaughlin and Dr. Steady provided important guidance on the editing and organization of the book. UNIFEM's Editorial Advisory Committee members Dorienne Rowan Campbell and Virginia Vargas also offered valuable insights. We also want to thank Marjorie Thorpe, then UNIFEM Deputy Director, for her support and literary critique.

Special thanks go to Joanne Sandler and Sushma Kapoor of UNIFEM for their commitment and steadfast support in following up with the contributors and chipping in with research where necessary. In managing the editorial process, they have gone to great lengths to ensure that the quality and style of the text remain faithful to the spirit of the writers and the panels in Costa Rica.

Thanks are due to Jane Katz for her initial editing and continued advice on the manuscript; and to Michelle Travis who volunteered her time to transcribe many videotapes.

Last but not least, I want to thank most sincerely my colleague, Ana Maria Brasileiro, who not only collaborated with me in the sponsorship of the panels but also helped to ensure that the book reflects the breadth of the African diaspora and the burden of inequality that racism places on Black women globally.

Both Ana Maria and I remain indebted to the United Nations Development Fund for Women for the support and visibility accorded to this important, complex and sensitive development issue.

A. O. P.

Ana Maria Brasileiro

Preface

W hen I think back on my involvement with the beginnings of the women's movement in Latin America, I remember the discourse, the meetings, and the writing that often focused on our identity, our self-image, our self-esteem. What I also remember is that we operated from the assumption that when we talked about women's identities and women's self-esteem, we tended to talk about all women. In those early days, there was little understanding or acceptance of difference. The oppression of women was universal and we mobilized to raise awareness, confront patriarchy and change the systems that kept us subservient.

We have come a long way in our analysis and acknowledgement of the challenges and issues that accompany broad-based coalition and alliance building amongst women. This book, *Connecting Across Cultures and Continents,* is but one of a growing number of initiatives, worldwide, to build a more democratic movement; a movement that welcomes reflections on what separates us as well as our commonalities. Dialogue and confrontation about class, culture, race, ethnicity and religion have long been an essential part of building a women's movement. But in this last decade, we have seen these dialogues cross national and regional boundaries, we have seen the harder issues of resources and leadership within the movement enter the discourse, and we have seen the names and faces of the interlocutors change to create a more diverse and representative movement.

In publishing this book, UNIFEM is seeking to bring these dialogues and debates into the development arena. This book is consistent with our own institutional policy of giving voice to those who are frequently invisible to policy makers and planners, and of bringing to light issues that have yet to arrive at the negotiating tables of multilateral and bilateral organizations. As the writers in this volume articulate repeatedly, the triple or quadruple burdens that Black women face—because of their colour and gender, because of colonialism, because of their resulting poverty—transcend borders and cultures. It is the transcendent nature of this discrimination that we must all understand. It unifies the writers in this volume and the organizations and initiatives that they represent in spite of their geographic, language and historical differences.

It is our hope that the words and thoughts of the Black women who have contributed to this book will create awareness and understanding amongst men and women of all races and ethnicities who are committed to shaping an approach to development that is equitable and sustainable.

Ana Maria Brasileiro is chief of UNIFEM's Latin America and Caribbean Section. Born in Brazil, she is an early activist on women's issues in Latin America. She holds a doctorate degree in Political Science from the University of Essex, UK.

Achola O. Pala

Introduction

S hortly after settling into my new apartment in New York, I had a strange experience in the most ordinary of circumstances.

I was in the basement of my building doing my laundry. As I loaded the washing machine, a woman approached me and asked, "Are you available to do some work for me? I need someone for a few hours." Confused, I replied, "I work in the city." She didn't understand what I was saying and responded, "I need someone to work for me." Then it dawned on me. I said, "Gosh, I need someone to work for me too. Do you know anyone I can hire?" She looked at me in utter amazement and went on sorting her laundry.

Because I am Black, she assumed I was a domestic worker. That I was a Harvard Ph.D., and working at the UN were unthinkable to my neighbour. She saw only my dark skin. To her, that sufficiently defined my identity.

Black people, (dis)placed in all corners of the globe in the African diaspora, are well-acquainted with such thoughtless racism. Our individual odysseys are shaped by our time in history, our circumstances, and our locations. Many of us in the diaspora have experienced the bitter taste of repeated and prolonged discrimination and have come to internalize racist categories and descriptions of ourselves. No Black woman escapes unscathed. In Africa as well, Africans have faced such discrimination in the context of colonialism and its legacies. The experience of the diaspora demonstrates the commonalities shared by Africans worldwide.

Even in the development discourse today, where the well-being of every inhabitant on this planet is the supposed goal, racism continues to be a dirty secret. Public discussion on racial discrimination is charged with emotion. A great deal of fear surrounds an honest examination of the underpinnings of racial discrimination. Therefore ambivalence persists, and racial discrimination as a development issue goes unchallenged.

Indeed, few in the international development community are prepared to plumb the depths of racial discrimination and how it affects the opportunities and possibilities for Black people, especially Black women. Just as discrimination on the basis of gender is being challenged as a fundamental denial of women's humanity, discrimination on the basis of race should be challenged since it constitutes a fundamental denial of the humanity of Black people.

To challenge discrimination of any kind, to realize the full meaning of equity and development, it is essential that people who have been discriminated against speak out and peel back societies' layers of discrimination. At a personal level, this is the essential step in self-definition, in creating a mirror for ourselves into which we can announce: "This is who we are, where we come from, where we're going." Until we in development understand things from the excluded people's perspective, until we can see their reflection in their own mirror, we can never have a new society. We therefore have a collective responsibility to continue to interrogate the basis of inequality, and the means and methods by which exclusion happens. We must reject exclusion in all its forms.

As perhaps the supreme example of state-sanctioned racism, the Holocaust holds valuable lessons for those struggling against exclusion, destruction and genocide. Once we deepen our understanding of all aspects of the Holocaust, particularly of how discrimination leads to de-humanization and to genocide, we can take steps to insist that we never return to the extreme horror of targeted, deliberate racial destruction.

Given the world's espoused interest in democracy, human rights, and women's rights, now is the time for the international development community to set the stage for Black women to present their reality—to define, in their own words, who they are and the world they want to live in. That is why *Connecting Across Cultures and Continents: Black Women Speak Out on Identity, Race and Development* was undertaken.

In February 1993, the United Nations Development Fund for Women (UNIFEM) sponsored two panels at the Fifth International Interdisciplinary Congress on Women in Costa Rica. The purpose was to focus attention on key issues in Black women's identities and livelihoods and to examine implications for the global women's movement. The collection of essays in this volume resulted from those two panels. Owing to geographic and cultural diversity within the global Black community itself, an effort was made to select a representative group of participants from different parts of the world to present the message of the Black woman as she sees her situation in varying regions and circumstances.

This global meeting of Black women was not the first of its kind. Two earlier encounters had taken place—one in Argentina in 1990 and another in the Dominican Republic in 1993—adding momentum to a Black women's consciousness movement. This movement led to the formation of a Global Black Women's Network. UNIFEM's role was to provide support and visibility to the ongoing efforts, and to bring the vision and experiences of the Black women to the development discussions at the United Nations.

My colleague Ana Maria Brasileiro and I saw the Fifth World Congress on Women, being held for the first time in a developing country, as a good forum for raising persisting challenges to sustainable development. We believed then and now that a critique of discrimination on the basis of race, just as discrimination on the basis of gender, must start with those who are most adversely affected. For Black women, it is often one and the same. We also believed that by forcing ourselves to look into the abyss of exclusion, we are able to initiate ourselves into an appreciation of diversity. With this starts the tiny step towards understanding those elements of discrimination that have gone so deep by listening to the people who have experienced it.

The papers in this volume examine the concept of Black identity from both Northern and Southern perspectives—from Canada to the Caribbean, from Germany to Nigeria, from South Africa to Brazil—and offer a critique of the dominant paradigm against which we struggle in order to gain that self-definition. While the essays refocus attention on the persisting problem of racism as a challenge to international development, they sound a call to the international women's movement to support Black women's efforts to scale the obstacles of exclusion and realize their own humanity, and to provide a pathway for Black women in the international women's agenda.

As a history of ideas, mainstream feminist literature looks at womanhood in the context of European cultural history. In the North there are increasing efforts to undertake and disseminate the analysis and understanding of what the Black experience teaches us, both in regard to issues confronting feminists and in regard to the need for solidarity in international movements. However, poor access to the publishing markets continues to limit the global circulation of writings by Black feminists. Moreover, unresolved tensions around the supremacy of ideas inhibit opportunities to integrate Black women's participation in the international women's movement. Even where Black women writers have provided alternative analysis, it has not become the main referent in the feminist debate. This volume of papers is crucial in broadening the cross-cultural feminist imagination. It provides visibility for Black women's networks, as represented by the individual authors who themselves have been engaged in delineating both the context and the experience of their exclusion. It also provides visibility to the scholarship on Black women and contributes to the history of ideas on feminism.

Similarly, for African people, the opportunity to share the scholarship about African heritage and African resistance to colonial domination and racism is empowering to both those who impart knowledge and those who receive it. Through study and analysis of their specific condition and social institutions, Africans around the world can forge an image of themselves that validates their reality, builds their self-esteem and confidence, and acknowledges their contributions to global human development.

Black women have to be understood in the context of their cumulative history, their resistance to oppression, their ongoing experiences, and as carriers of culture. What defines womanhood in the culture into which they were born can be totally transformed by moving into another culture. What often then appears is a person truncated from the definition that, in some sense, protected and defined her humanity.

Each and every essay in this volume is an affirmation of Black women's identity. The wide-ranging presentations provide a continuum, with Africa as the source of the original home of Black folk, and examine the changes that have come about in gender roles as Africans travelled into the diaspora. The authors examine the conflicting environments in which Black women's identity has faced a continual interrogation by the dominant cultures, piecing together elements of the historic past and present, and of public and private information to paint the significance of this experience and the resilience of Black people.

Several papers here focus on the creativity of Black women and their fighting spirit, particularly as displayed by maroon women who provided organized challenges to enslavement and frustrated the attempts of slavers to dehumanize Africans. "Black Women and Identity in the Caribbean: Out of the Quagmire" by Eintou Pearl Springer delves into history to show that Black people resisted racism and slavery from the beginning and continued to build the resistance movement and a revolutionary consciousness to challenge racism. Springer cites the arranged escapes, feigned madness, suicide and even infanticide as means to resist captivity. Springer concludes that such dysfunctional albeit courageous practices, which slaves adopted to avoid the torture and dehumanization of captivity, gave rise to the phenomenon of self-loss.

Another facet of self-loss is evident in African women's entrapment in the beauty bind. Glenda Simms' "From Fractured Identities, a New Consciousness" explores beauty with an eye to the problems that young Black women face. In dominant, Western cultures, Simms points out, the Snow White phenomena has perpetuated a perception that polarizes dark and light. Complexion then becomes linked to class and virtue. Furthermore, with the introduction of market-based consumerism, women were forced to redefine their beauty in terms of light and dark. Simms contends that beauty as a commodity undermines a woman's essential being by imposing new—and often unrealistic—definitions of attractiveness upon her.

One's role in society, and society's perception of that role, also play a part in crafting identity. In this vein, several contributors point to the need for alternative concepts and analytical frameworks that more accurately assess the economic contribution of women to society. "Gender-responsive Agenda for Equitable Development" by Felicia Ekejiuba pointedly questions the analytical paradigm that identifies the "household" as the unit of production and consumption in statistical and social analysis. When the narrow concept of "household" is used in configuring a woman's role in society, it brings with it an inbuilt notion of dependency on the male as the head of the house. It conjures up the image of the woman as being totally subordinated by the man in her reproductive, service and consumer role, and it considers her work of no value. Ekejiuba constructs the brilliant analytic concept of the "hearthold," a female-centred unit of consumption as well as production. When looked at from the vantage point of the hearthold as opposed to the household, the woman is seen not as a consumer of what the man bestows but as a provider on many levels. It is this range of roles and the structural value of women in female farming systems that characterize Africa's social economies and that give African women their sense of esteem as mothers, food suppliers, daughters of the village and as people in their own right who are not submerged in the faceless and devalued household. Ekejiuba proves that by looking at indigenous African concepts, of which the hearthold is but one example, the portrait of female identity and autonomy that emerges can be startlingly opposed to the traditional view.

Racism is a historical phenomena. Therefore the strategies for combating it have to take into account the historical context in which racism thrives. Danisa Baloyi's "Apartheid and Identity: Black Women in South Africa," dealing with the situation of Black women under state sanctioned racism, draws attention to the triple or even quadruple discrimination of race, class, gender and culture. "Power, Racism and Identity" by Sergia Galvan, charting the complex interrelationship between the historical, social, political and cultural variables, offers insight into the evolution of Black women's identity in Latin America. Sueli Carneiro, in "Defining Black Feminism," emphasizes the need for Black women's organizations to create and strengthen their own intellectual and analytical space.

Feminist strategies change within national and regional contexts. "The Impact of the Black Consciousness and Women's Movements on Black Women's Identity: Intercontinental Empowerment" by Andrée McLaughlin presents the global dimension of Black women's organizations and reports on the growing Black women's consciousness movement. With personal testimonies of Black women from different parts of the diaspora, McLaughlin confirms that Black identity mirrors the range of historical circumstances and priorities of different groups. Adopted in different ways by exploited or oppressed peoples for social, economic, and political power, Black identity has represented a practical alliance to evolve common political strategies.

The linkage between economic exploitation and racial discrimination is a theme that is recognized by all the contributors. "Women in the Caribbean: The Quadruple Burden of Gender, Race, Class and Imperialism" by Peggy Antrobus expands on the issue by focusing on the relationship between poverty, class and racism. According to Antrobus, social differentiation arises from the incorporation of Blacks as well as Asians into a capitalist labour market that attempts to justify exploitation of the enslaved or indentured labour. In this market system, poor Black women are the most exploited population.

Antrobus echoes the fact that studies of women in the Caribbean have often shown how the extraction of male labour in plantation agriculture has discriminated against women in the same way that commercial plantation agriculture discriminated against women in Africa. First, it extracts male labour by incorporating men more systematically into the labour market. Then it isolates women by not remunerating their labour or devaluing it by confining it to the role of merely supporting the males entering paid labour. The irony, Antrobus points out, is that at the same time that the restructuring redefines categories of labour by gender, it also devalues both female and male labour because of racism. Thus even though the man enters the paid labour force, he is only superficially freed by it since the wages he receives are not equal to the value of his labour, and it continues to confine him to the lower rungs of society. Women's labour is also diminished and exploited by the same process.

Travelling in the Americas, the Caribbean and the African continent itself, one is struck by the effect of post-colonial economic and cultural conditions that have attempted to dehumanize and destroy the social and economic bases of Black society. Yet paradoxically, the trauma of subjugation has not led to total despair. Instead it has produced an insistent interrogation and resistance by Black people all over the world. This volume provides an opportunity to uncover the complex issues surrounding the identity of Black women globally. These essays offer linkages for people in the process of reclaiming their identity. I believe they help provide a means of validating one's personhood. I believe the voices in this collection provide a public tribunal in which racism can and must be openly interrogated. If people do not have some control over the definition of their own identity, then they simply cannot be. And to be is to identify yourself. If you are unable to do that, you flounder in the abyss of exclusion.

The dialogues in this book provide a cross-cultural, multidisciplinary critique of racism and discriminatory practices from Black women's perspective. As such, they seek to enrich the international development discourse. They also seek to widen the feminist imagination worldwide and to command a space in the international women's movement.

That movement has a collective responsibility to call racism to shame. UNIFEM's objective is to ensure that all marginalized women are able to enter the debate about their future so that they can secure a place in the international women's movement that will enable them to change the conditions that keep them poor. UNIFEM joins the women of the world in advocating for change. Women are demanding new pathways to development for sustainable and secure livelihoods, stable lives and power sharing not just for women but for all people. Women are indeed setting a new agenda for the 21st century. The world community must rethink the development project afresh.

Achola O. Pala is chief of UNIFEM's Africa Section. Born in Kenya, she is known for her work on women, gender, and the social transformation of African cultures and societies. She received an M.A. in Education and a Ph.D. in Anthropology from Harvard University, USA.

Sueli Carneiro

Defining Black Feminism

---

hold the reflections of the past so
we will never go that way again
             – Johari M. Amini from
               "Story for the Remainder"

Sueli Carneiro is the coordinator of the Human Rights and
Racial Equality Programme (SOS-RACISMO) of Geledés—
Instituto da Mulher Negra in São Paulo and co-founder of the
International Feminist Network for Black Women's Studies.

"We are women who, for centuries, have worked as slaves on farms and as whores on city streets; as salespersons behind shop counters; and as caretakers behind strangers' doors....Ours is the contingent of women who have not understood a word when feminists said that women should go out of their homes and work!" – Sueli Carneiro

Every person comes into the world with a biologically determined gender and racial identity. On the basis of these two factors, we inherit a social identity. How we *feel* about that identity depends on historical, cultural, religious and psychological elements. This can be unfortunate for more than half the world's people because of the simple fact that these elements are constructs of opposition.

For example, being identified as female is often defined as not being male. From a physical point of view, the female is said to be inferior to the male because she lacks the male's physical strength; from a religious point of view, the female is seen as less than the male, having been created from Adam's rib; from a cultural standpoint, she is a second-class citizen relegated to a specific and severely limited arena, since she is excluded from the more privileged male sphere.

All these characterizations lead to a negative identity for the female. Attempts are made not only to justify this subordination and oppression of women but also to foist upon women themselves acceptance of their socially subordinate role.

The first wave of the feminist movement in Brazil and elsewhere expressed deep indignation regarding this oppression, and the movement concentrated on repudiating existing stereotypes about women. The movement targeted the myth of female fragility; the confinement of women within the home; the limiting notion of women as mere reproductive agents. Creating a positive female identity is an ongoing effort that first requires dismantling the model of woman as the home queen, the myth of the implacable destiny of motherhood, and the centuries of domination by the male and patriarchal ideology.

In the second stage, the movement recognized the need to provide full citizenship for women in order to create a new female identity. Building on work from the first phase of the movement, when the focus was on breaking down stereotypes, women have united around several issues and have articulated their needs strongly:

• If we accept that men and women can do the same jobs, we must strive to ensure that women earn the same as men for equal work and that women have access to high-skill jobs.

• If we accept that gender makes no difference in terms of the type of work we are capable of, formal education in schools should be made to end the stereotyping that leads girls towards activities regarded as female activities. We should recognize the shortcomings of gender-biased materials and promote gender equality in school books and other teaching instruments.

• If we accept that a biological difference is not a disadvantage, we should question our roles as women, mothers, teachers, etc., to seek a response to the discriminatory ideology against women's productive and reproductive roles.

• If we accept that biological differences between men and women point to unique concerns at the health level, we need to promote a programme for women's health that recognizes the different phases of a woman's life from puberty to post-menopause. The programme should acknowledge that different cycles experienced by women require distinct health approaches.

• If we accept that having or not having children should be a matter of choice determined by a woman or a couple, we must demand that the Government make available to women several contraceptive methods along with accurate and objective information about each method. We must demand an end to the calamity of massive sterilization of women, unnecessary caesarean operations, and clandestine abortions, which are responsible for the death of countless women.

• If we accept that women have the right to control their own reproduction, we should influence the policy debates and the public health system which regard women, particularly those of the lower classes, as being too ignorant to use the contraceptive methods available, and which induce them to use methods such as IUDs. All of these prevent women from taking charge of their own health.

• If we accept that the subjugation of women has permitted men to inflict violence against us without punishment, we must insist that domestic violence and rape cease to be viewed as a private matter and that they instead become a social and cultural problem that society will not tolerate.

• If we accept that the subordination of women allows the creation of discriminatory laws against them, we must argue for laws that protect women's rights under the new Constitution.

The forging of a female identity depends on securing full citizenship for women. But the question that still remains is whether the above list of rights will assure full citizenship to all Brazilian women.

The Colour of Feminism

We talk about dismantling the myth of female fragility that has historically justified the paternalistic protection men provide women. However, when we discuss female fragility, let us stop to ask: which women are we talking about? As Black women, we are part of a contingent that has never been treated as fragile. We are women who, for centuries, have worked as slaves on farms and as whores on city streets; as salespersons behind shop counters; and as caretakers behind strangers' doors. Yesterday we were at the service of delicate young ladies and sadistic sugar-mill lords; today, we are the maids of liberated women, or we are export-type 'mulatas'. Ours is the contingent of women who have not understood a word when feminists said that women should go out of their homes and work!

When we speak about shattering the home-queen myth or about smashing the pedestalled muse worshipped by poets, which women are we talking to? Black women are part of a contingent of women who are queens of nothing, who are portrayed as the anti-heroes of Brazilian society because the aesthetic ideal for women is patterned after the white female.

When we talk about assuring equal opportunities for men and women in the job market, to which women are we making that proposal? We are part of a contingent of women whose education precludes us from the very notion of equal opportunity at work.

When we talk about raising awareness about women's health, which women do we have in mind? We are part of a contingent of women ignored by the health system because the myth of racial democracy generally does not require collecting data according to the colour of patients—information indispensable in assessing and managing the health of Black women in Brazil. As we know through data from other countries, white and Black women are subjected to different health risks, and therefore have different health needs requiring distinct treatments.

Our reproductive potential has received special attention. The massive sterilization of Black women has been suggested by government advisors based on the reasoning that if the growth of the Black population is not restrained, by the year 2000 we would constitute an absolute majority and would be able to compete for the political control of the country.

The classical discourse on the oppression of women does not take into account the qualitative difference of oppression endured by Black women and the effect it had and still has on our identity and our participation in society.

To speak of a female identity implies recognizing that beyond the sexual aspect, an essential factor in any discussion of identity is the racial aspect. Fifty per cent of the women's faces in my country are Black, and they confront a specific type of oppression, namely, racial violence, a characteristic of Brazilian society.

The level of inequality existing between the white and Black women in Brazil is an indication of the social distance between Black women and the remaining sectors of the society. The social inequalities in terms of education, participation in the formal job market, and monthly earnings, etc., are profound.

Concerning access to education, the data published as of the 1980 census is startling: the illiteracy rate among Black women is around 48 per cent, while it drops to 24 per cent among white women.

Average monthly earnings also vary significantly according to the colour of the individual. While 85 per cent of Black women live below the poverty level, the figure is 64 per cent for white women.

The level of social unbalance between white and Black women is replicated between Black men and Black women. Clearly, the achievements of the feminist movement have been more to the benefit of white women, and the achievements of the Black movement tend to benefit the Black man, leaving Black women in the abysmal position of being lowest in Brazil's social hierarchy.

Black Women Organizing

This social strangulation is giving rise to organizations of Black women whose purpose is to develop strategies of their own in order to fight racial and sexual discrimination aimed against Black women.

However, for this double militancy to be effective, a third goal is required: the independent organization of Black women as a political force capable of discussing partnership on equal terms with the Black movement, the women's movement, and other organized sectors of society.

Geledés, the Black Women's Institute, an organization to which I belong, was created with the goal of fighting racial and sexual discrimination. We believe Black women must take responsibility for raising political questions that speak to their situation in society. They must be outspoken regarding questions affecting society in general and the Black population in particular.

To achieve this, the Institute has set up three basic programmes: Human

Rights and Racial Equality, Health, and Communication. Through these programmes we attempt to act simultaneously on the question of women's rights and on racism.

The purpose of the Human Rights Programme is to fight all forms of violation against the Black population through actions and proposals intended to ensure the full exercise of such human rights. The Institute addresses racial discrimination through information campaigns, institutional interventions and legal assistance.

The overall purpose of the Health Programme is to disseminate information regarding reproduction, and mental and general health, with specific reference to the Brazilian Black woman. The programme also organizes discussion sessions and workshops, trains community leaders, and lobbies on behalf of Black women with public and private health institutions.

In the area of mental health, the programme sponsors the "Building Our Solidarity" project. From our personal and collective experience, we realize that racism and sexism have an extremely powerful influence on our emotional development. Violence caused by racism and sexism often translates into pain, anger, impotence and shame, making us feel inferior to white women and to men. This project offers support to other Black women. We are also forming self-help groups to provide opportunities for meetings of Black women to share experiences. At present we have 12 groups with a total of about 100 Black women who meet every fortnight.

As a non-governmental organization, we have been acting in partnership with several organizations to create public policies that aim to eliminate all forms of discrimination suffered by women and Black people in Brazilian society. The Institute's management is composed exclusively of Black women; however, its various work teams have been cooperative efforts staffed by men and women, both Black and white.

To make a difference in the lives of Brazilian Black women, we have more to do than just hope for a better future, a future where female identity is prized for its own characteristics, which are not defined in contradiction to male characteristics. What we have to do is to organize, and to never stop questioning. What we have to do, as always, is plenty of work.

2

Eintou Pearl Springer

Black Women and Identity in the Caribbean: Out of the Quagmire

A good deal of time and intelligence has been invested in the exposure of racism and horrific results on its objects.... But that well-established study should be joined with another, equally important one: the impact of racism on those who perpetuate it.

— Toni Morrison

Poet, actress and playwright Eintou Pearl Springer was born in Santa Cruz, Trinidad. She has published three collections of her poetry and has been featured in various anthologies. She is a founding member and co-director of the Caribbean Theatre Guild and has adapted Caribbean novels for the stage. Currently she holds the post of Librarian-in-Charge of the West Indian Reference Library, Port-of-Spain.

"The question of identity is at the very fulcrum of Black existence. It demands that the Black woman's struggle for visibility and recognition be carried out on a par with her role and responsibilities within the context of her community and her race."

— *Eintou Pearl Springer*

"Like the Caribbean region itself, like the poor, and especially like the African man of her region, the Caribbean woman has had to struggle against an imposed 'invisibility' compounded by stereotypes and misrepresentation. A region which is rich, important and remarkably creative is presented as poor, unimportant, dependent, exotic, a tourist playground, a great power's backyard. Similarly the Caribbean woman: survivor, creator and preserver of culture, tireless worker and indomitable fighter is presented to the world in a series of stereotypes in which she is rendered as a mere object."[1]

The Historical Perspective

The Caribbean has failed to have a meaningful encounter with the history of the people who comprise the greatest number of its inhabitants. That failure has denied Africans in the Caribbean the ability to move forward and achieve the social transformation that would provide solutions to the region's problems.

The quagmire of domination and self-loss in which the Black diaspora flounders is real for both the African man and the African woman. The question of identity is at the very fulcrum of Black existence. It demands that the Black woman's struggle for visibility and recognition be carried out on a par with her role and responsibilities within the context of her community and her race.

It is essential to look at the history that the Caribbean region has failed so far to confront. Though there is ample documentary evidence supporting the presence of African peoples in this part of the world as far back as 800 B.C., most Africans came to the Caribbean as enslaved peoples between 1600 and 1870. One third were females, ranging in age from 14 to 40. They were already grounded in their culture, and they were willing to fulfil all the roles expected of them in the traditional society.

During this period of enslavement in the Caribbean, women resisted in ways both active and passive. Resistance began even on the way to the Caribbean. Our enslaved mothers—daughters of Candace, Nzinga, Makeda, and Yaa Asantewa—committed suicide and attempted escape as alternatives to dealing with the horror of enslavement. On the plantation, the African woman was "equal under the whip," and was involved in every facet of plantation work. Lady Nugent, wife of the governor of Jamaica, wrote in her journal, which she kept during her residence in Jamaica from 1801 to 1805, "Women with child, work in the fields till the last six weeks, and are at work there again in a fortnight after the confinement."[2]

The Black woman, prey of the white man and of his Black overseers, was consistently subjected to rape. The Black man, forced into a situation where he could neither protect nor provide for his womenfolk, saw his manhood atrophy. The sexual myths evolved. One of those that continues to bedevil us is the concept of the forbidden white woman as the ultimate ideal of beauty. The myths endure, shackled by lack of self-love. In the maelstrom, deprived of protection and providence, the Black woman sank deep into her self and found the will to resist—a will that still characterizes the Caribbean Black woman. She poisoned 'massa'; snuffed out the life of her newborn infant, holding tiny nostrils between her fingers or keeping a tiny head beneath water; she still-birthed the cries that would have come from newborn enslaved lips by powerful herbal abortifacients, often, in the process, giving her own life.

In maroonage, or in guerilla warfare, she shone.[3] Resistance of all kinds was active and passive. Running away constituted an act signalling that the human spirit could never be completely enslaved. Some were even willing to give their very lives, in the pursuit of their right to be humans instead of chattel. A woman's name is mentioned in every uprising; for example, Nanny Gregg of Barbados, and Cubah, elected queen of the city of Kingston, and hanged for such presumption.

The so-called Amelioration Bill of 1823 proposed the prohibition of the flogging of female slaves and the freedom of female children born after 1823. The plantocracy objected strenuously to the very thought of these women of an "Amazonian cast of character" going unpunished.

In 1825 and the following year, Woodford, Governor of Trinidad and Tobago, in his reports to the Colonial Secretary in London, cites frequent cases of insolence and insubordination among the female slaves. In Trinidad, records show that between 1824 and 1826, nearly twice as many women as men had to be punished. "The violence of turbulent women" and the "provoking tongues and noises of women" are two of the phrases that Lucille Mathurin uses to describe them in her book, *The Rebel Woman*.[4] A survey of cases in the magistrate's courts in Jamaica between 1819 and 1835 found words like "insulting," "abusive," "threatening" and "outrageous" frequently applied to the Black woman.

The Post-Emancipation Era
In the aftermath of enslavement, in the coming of the freedom for which Black men and Black women had striven with Ogun's machete and Kwaku Anansi's guile, the Black woman began to rebuild her family. In the post-emancipation era the Black man searched for his shrivelled self, and his weight was hers too. When she left the plantation, she became the backbone of the Caribbean peasantry. She bore the Black man on her back, and in her belly, buoyed by the remnants of her culture and strengthened by the very fact of her survival.

She made starch, handicrafts, cassava bread, coconut oil; she planted food, organized the marketing; she was huckster, broke the stones for macadamizing public roads, and cut cane. All this she did despite the denial of good land, despite lack of capital and transport. And she remained in the forefront of open rebellion. Sarah Frances was executed for her part in the Morant Bay uprising of 1865. In *The History of the Guyanese Working Class*, Walter Rodney documents the full participation of working class women in the 1905 rebellion: "Of the 105 persons convicted in the Georgetown Magistrates Court as a result of the riots 41 were female."[5]

The Carriers of the Culture
The deliberate attempt to divorce the enslaved Africans from their culture was relentlessly pursued. It ranged from the suppression of religion, language, music and musical instruments to forbidding the traditional method of giving birth. The destruction of the African family was central to this attempt at reversing their cultural affinities.

Family groups were separated by being sold to different plantations. Unions were unstable since all slaves were chattel and could be sold at any time. Children belonged to 'massa' and could be disposed of as he so chose. Members of the same language group were also separated. All this was done to discourage rebellion.

However, much more of the culture has survived than has been generally recognized. There is a well-entrenched myth that Black people became totally removed from their culture. The evidence does not, however, support this. A body of material collected by researchers such as Orlando Patterson, Melville Herskovits, Maureen Warner-Lewis and J.D. Elder documents the great degree of survival of many elements of African culture in the areas of food, language, dress, ritual and religion. Our women, forced to assume sole responsibility for the family, also had to assume the role of the carriers of this culture.

The fight for the preservation of the culture was recognized as germane to resistance. Mathurin reports that the maroon leader Nanny "greeted with great bitterness the news in 1739 of the male maroon leader Cudjoe's peace treaty with the English and ordered the execution of the white soldier who brought her the message."[6] It is significant that as the men signed the truce, the women stood by wearing defiantly round their ankles as ornaments the teeth of the white soldiers they had killed in battle!

Rebellious slaves mistrusted those who became Europeanized. They condemned those women who grew to love the masters' children they had been forced to suckle, and those who, male and female, began to concur in the myth of their own inferiority. It was a primary rule of maroonage—in Surinam, Brazil, Jamaica, St. Vincent, Belize—that rebels live away from the influence of white culture and according to the old ways.

The Aftermath

During the period of enslavement, African culture provided a psychological device for coping. There was the satire of songs, the duality of personhood (through story-telling) and the religious syncretism that allowed the slaves access to their God.

The mother-headed household evolved as the woman assumed the responsibility for her family following the destruction of the institution of paternity. She found, within her race and genetic memory, the concepts of matrilineality practiced by most West African peoples and adapted it to her Caribbean situation to create matrifocal households. She was supported by the extended family and the elders. She fought, she survived, but most important, she nurtured and loved with legendary selflessness.

Nevertheless, the values of the dominant Eurocentric cultures infiltrated her psyche, as they infiltrated that of her man. The destruction of language and religion and the seeming erosion of the memory of any pre-enslavement history have taken a toll, creating a serious schizophrenia. All this has produced a people from African roots to whom the notion of things African is loathsome, even while they still, in so many ways, live the African culture; a people whose God is represented in the image of their historical oppressors; a people from whom physical chains have been removed but whose minds still remain enchained by the recent history of domination, self-loss, and continuing cultural and economic imperialisms.

Our economies are now shackled to the IMF and the World Bank. When a Black baby dies from cholera or gastro-enteritis because monies that should go to health services must service debt repayment, there is a need to understand that economic repression continues. In the wake of the IMF and World Bank stranglehold on Caribbean economies, massive retrenchment and high prices have affected family life and further exacerbated the identity crises. Most Black families in the Caribbean are poor by European and North American standards. Yet, their distrust of the agendas of official agencies causes them to largely ignore family planning and have families they can ill-afford to support. Women's health continues to be affected by hard work, stress, and frequent childbirth. In a poverty-ridden environment, children are a poor man's/woman's wealth; for women, the preoccupation with children can fill the need to bolster her self-worth. But the impoverishment of her people can be no salve to the Black woman's self-image.

Culture, Economics and Identity

Cultural imperialism brings into her home, through the one-eyed monster, an alien lifestyle and a culture that glorifies sex and violence. She lives the reality of poverty and escapes to alien affluence every night. The technology that is creating the global village, and the satellites overhead, are not mere machines. They are, in fact, imbued with the values of those who own and control the means of production. The Black Caribbean woman is caught in the dilemma of being entitled, on the one hand, to the finest products of the human mind and, on the other, experiencing a deepening of the identity schism resulting from that very technology.

In fact, it seems that the Black woman as carrier of the culture is very often forced to choose between fossilized customs and cultural imperialism. There is a notion that since emancipation, the culture has stagnated into simply providing coping devices.

Fanon has said, "Culture has never the translucidity of custom; it abhors all simplification. In its essence it is opposed to custom, for custom is always the deterioration of culture. The desire to attach oneself to tradition or bring abandoned traditions to life again, does not only mean going against the current of history but also opposing one's own people."[7]

The African woman in the Caribbean invested heavily in education in the post-emancipation era. The curriculum, however, has not addressed the need to deal with the identity crisis. It has not begun to mirror the rights of the Afro-Caribbean people, or teach a history of resistance rather than victimhood, or stress that the period of enslavement was but a short chapter in a long and glorious history. In the countries of the North, efforts are now being made to give Africa its rightful place in world history. In the Caribbean, the role that education must play has still not been recognized.

In many instances, educating the children has meant losing them in terms of traditional values and cultural links. In fact, tertiary education in the Caribbean was established with a deliberate agenda to 'separate the best from the rest.' As Ronald Reagan's infamous Santa Fe document states, "Education is the medium by which culture retains, passes on, and even pioneers history. Thus whoever controls the educational system determines the past, how it is conceived, as well as the future."

Education has not equipped the largely male political leadership in the region to deal with the identity crisis, or to affect the social transformation necessary within the region. What it has equipped them with is a perfect neocolonial model of functioning. Not only in politics and economics does the identity crisis bedevil us; the effects are equally devastating in two other critical areas—religion and relationships.

Our women flee to the panacea of religion. Black women are the bulwark of Christian religions. It is the Black women who maintain the churches with their hard work and almost orgasmic fervour. In the male-dominated Christian hierarchy, women do the work but receive neither power nor recognition. There is the continuing anomaly of Black women praying zealously, following the biblical injunction to be "whiter than snow." All societies create their own God in their own image. The African woman, however, kneels and hopes to find salvation in a God that is the colour of her oppressor. African religions have been particularly stigmatized. It is no wonder that the only successful slave revolution in Caribbean history was in Haiti where the traditional religion was dominant. The Haitians followed the God of their ancestors. His cast of features, hue of skin, and perception of the world paralleled their own. He propelled them to victory, galled by the denial of the humanity of his devotees; and his anger was terrible, his vengeance slaked only by the dull thud of the machete.

Sometimes it appears that Black men and Black women live in a state of being at war with each other. Damaged by history, many Black men still look for a white woman; many consistently ill-treat the Black woman and ignore their children. The woman, cut off from the extended family that nurtured her in the post-emancipation era, and even on the plantation, must in many instances face all the problems of society alone—without sexual fulfilment, the support of a mate, or the closeness and companionship of a warm and caring relationship.

Out of the Quagmire

It seems that it is the ceaseless task of Black women in the Caribbean to be the burden bearer of the race. Black women—as mothers, as teachers, as carriers of the culture—have a responsibility to recognize and deal with this identity crisis that continues to cripple us. Our vulnerability to economic and cultural oppression is directly linked to our history and the question of identity. It is only our recognition, acceptance, and love of who we are that can help us to revolutionize our stance in every facet of our lives. The food we eat, the clothes we wear, where our children go to school are all crucial political decisions that reflect our sense of self.

It is time, in the Caribbean, that Black organizations insist that the education system reflect the reality of African history and the history of the African in the Caribbean in a way that would contribute to the positive self-image of African men and women.

It is time, within Black organizations and Black communities, that the crisis of male-female relationships be discussed and analyzed with a view to nurturing mutual respect. The crisis in Black families, the attraction of drugs and crime to so many Black youths, and their seeming lack of direction are all linked to the identity crisis and a lack of ideological direction.

It is time that the Black woman works to give status and energy to the traditional religions. In so doing she will help to remove one of the most vicious causes of her personality schism, her involvement with Eurocentric religions.

It is time that the Black woman in the Caribbean unshackles her palate, frees her mind, and develops tastes that mirror her environment and her history.

It is time that education and a heightened sense of self fill the gap now being occupied by frequent childbearing.

It is time that the Black woman takes up the challenge of working to assist the development of cultural formulations that show respect and understanding of the past and that provide the opportunity to excise the elements of the traditional culture that are inimical to the development of her selfhood.

The Black women's movement, such as it is, needs to articulate this problem of identity and to force discussion and confrontation on this issue.

This then is the key—the question of identity within the context of the community. The Black woman in the Caribbean, as elsewhere in the diaspora, needs to solve the identity crisis alongside the Black man. Black men in the Caribbean suffer discrimination of class and race. Black women are additionally exploited on the basis of gender. It is her responsibility to deal, not only with gender issues, but those of race and class, even if this means bearing the burden of the race a while longer. Maybe by committing herself to bringing about a social transformation of the Caribbean region, and by confronting the identity crisis, this woman, this survivor, will in the process deal with her personal needs for recognition, visibility, and healed relationships. For surely, these questions are all intertwined.

[1] Cecil Gutzmore. 1986.
[2] Phillip Wright (Ed.). 1966.
[3] "Maroonage" refers to the decision to break the bonds of enslavement.
[4] Mathurin, L. 1975.
[5] Rodney, W. 1981.
[6] Mathurin, L. 1975.
[7] Fanon, F. 1967.

LINKS

There is a verse
running through my head,
it will not let me sleep
it drives me from my bed.

It is a verse
crying out against
my invisibility,
longing to testify,
to my humanity.

And the verse
stretches
to a poem.

There is a string
to my navel bound,
reaching for the sky
while rooted in the ground.

It is a string
buried in warm rich earth,
giving me just claim
to the land
of my birth.

And the string
tugs
at my heart.

There is a thread
reaching round the earth;
knitting scattered children
to whom the same mother
gave birth.

It is a thread
knotted and ancient,
stained, but still
resilient.

And the thread
knows the smell
of black blood.

There is a line
going back in time,
to great civilizations
I must claim as mine.
It is a line
telling the story
that leads me
to self discovery.

And the line
has the measure
of all time.

There is the earth
on which I walk proud,
knowing its fertility
is nurtured by my blood.

It is an earth
savaged by man,
destroying his heritage
by his own hand.

And the earth
will wreak vengeance
on mankind.

There is a fire
raging in my being.
waiting to lash out at all
who wish me to be unseen.

It is a fire
hot and wild, that will not be put
out
even,
when I die.

For that fire
burns
for freedom.

— **Eintou Pearl Springer**
From *Focussed*, a volume of poems
          by Springer, 1991.

Glenda Simms

From Fractured Identities, a New Consciousness

Ojo pa mi, ojo ko pa ewa ara mi danu.

The rain beats on me, but the rain cannot wash off the beauty of my body.

— Yoruba proverb

Dr. Glenda Simms is President of the Canadian Advisory
Council on the Status of Women and past president of the
Congress of Black Women of Canada. Originally from Jamaica,
Dr. Simms came to Canada to teach in 1966. She has had a
long-standing involvement with women, racial minorities,
Aboriginal peoples and community issues.

"The struggle for the Black diasporic identity in all racist societies is a continuing and universal theme. Why is this so? I think the answer lies in the crucial link between the historical and the contemporary." – Glenda Simms

Aspects of Oppression

The contemporary experiences of Black women in Canada demonstrate the unique challenges facing women of the diaspora living in white societies. Marginalized socially, economically, culturally, and politically they must forge a new consciousness from fractured identities.

The first Black person on record in Canada, Matthieu Da Costa, travelled as an interpreter with the 16th-century French explorer Samuel de Champlain. Today it is estimated that nearly half a million of a total population of 27 million Canadians are Black. Culturally and linguistically diverse, Black Canadians comprise a growing and vibrant force in the society.

From the earliest times Black people settled all across Canada—in areas as diverse as Alberta, Saskatchewan, Southern Ontario and Nova Scotia—as individuals, as families and as communities. Women comprised at least 50 per cent of these early populations. Like all pioneers, these women and their families persevered amidst harsh geographic conditions, poor economic realities, and isolation. Many more Black people came to Canada as British Empire Loyalists and as slaves. Later, others committed to freedom and the search for dignity braved the threat of capture and death to join the freedom train that brought runaway slaves to Canada from the United States. Also joining the movement of Black peoples to Canada were the maroons, who have a unique place in the history of our people.[1]

At the turn of this century, many other Black people from the Caribbean, amongst whom were schoolteachers and technicians, settled primarily in Montreal and Halifax. Once they arrived in Canada, however, the women worked as maids and as baby-sitters while the men swept floors and worked on the trains. The qualifications they had earned in their home country did not carry weight in the new environment.

Over the past 30 years many more have joined the third wave of immigrants in response to Canada's call for educated and skilled workers. These included domestic workers, professionals, students, farm workers, refugees, and well-qualified tradespeople. As a result, Black people have made sterling contributions as nurses and doctors in the hospitals in the major urban centres; as schoolteachers in remote communities; and as caregivers to the young and elderly. Many others have contributed to the public service and business sectors.

Having settled for many generations and having contributed in such meaningful ways to Canadian society, one would expect that Black women and, by extension, Black people, should have become an integral part of that society. This, however, is not the case. Today, Black women in general are amongst the most marginalized women in Canada. They share this distinction with Aboriginal Canadian women.

The struggle for the Black diasporic identity in all racist societies is a continuing and universal theme. Why is this so? I think the answer lies in the crucial link between the historical and the contemporary.

Black people in the United States, Great Britain and Canada share with Black people in South Africa and in Euro-dominated countries both the pain of white supremacist oppression and exploitation as well as the pain that comes from resistance and struggle. In examining the effects of history on the Black daughters of the diaspora, we have to continually analyze the blueprint of oppression constructed by colonial history. The chauvinism and greed that motivated the period after the "discovery" of the Caribbean and the so-called New World, and the succeeding period of colonialism have been explored by many Black writers, such as Orlando Patterson, Rex Nettleford, Frantz Fanon, Albert Memmi and Richard Wright to name but a few. The thrust of all this scholarship is that, whatever the rationale for the European invasion, the whites were positive that God was on their side. White was right; male was right; Christian was right.

Other writers, from V.S. Naipaul to Eric Williams, have documented the trauma and horror of the colonial period and the ensuing history of slavery in the Caribbean and Americas. Frederick Douglass' autobiography also remains a powerful statement on and description of the physical, social, economic and psychological nature of slavery and of the American slave society.

Angela Davis and other female writers have done much to clarify the effect of slavery on the Black female condition. Yet in spite of their eloquence, we simply cannot even begin to imagine the unspeakable horror of the slave experience—the moral and psychic decay, and the sheer physical carnage caused by colonialism and neo-colonialism on Black peoples of the world.

The diasporic Black woman has been relegated to the position of an immigrant worker, maid and the eternal mammy. She is the mother who is never worshipped as Madonna, the caretaker who is never respected as nurturer, the drudge who is never seen as artist or artisan, the woman who is never really a lady.

During the 1950s and 1960s, Canada imported 280 to 300 women yearly—predominantly from Jamaica, Barbados and Trinidad—to fill the labour-market need for domestic workers. Many of these women had been teachers, postal clerks, nurses and so on in their own country. The dramatic change they experienced from being a worker with some social status in their home country to a domestic worker in a foreign country reinforced the hierarchy of women and the stereotypes of Black women that originated during the era of slavery.

A Canadian writer, Dionne Brand, pointed out in her 1984 study of Black women in Toronto that Canadian Black women have always had to work as a condition of their race. The question is not that of the right to work, it is centred on the kind of work available to them.

One of the joint ironies of sexism and racism is that because of their gender, Black women find work in Canada—menial, low-paid, exhausting, and uncreative work in the "Pink-Collar Ghetto" or as domestics—while their men cannot. The sense of helplessness and rage produced by such ironies cannot be over-emphasized. Thus, the synergistic effect of oppression victimizes Black women in white society in ironic and cruel ways.

Standards of Desirability

Another important aspect of Black women's oppression is linked to the universal oppression of all women under patriarchy—the eternal search for "The Beautiful." This is a vicious cycle of victimization and alienation, abetted by the superimposition of a corrosive series of values of desirability and beauty that are damaging to Black women. "The Tyranny of Beauty," as I call this phenomenon, is that socio-cultural syndrome that teaches all women that it is preferable to be ill, malnourished, obsessed or dead rather than be considered ugly or undesirable.

Within Black groups, this tyranny of beauty is further complicated by the added factor of racist values concerning what is beautiful in a woman. This nexus of conflicting, denigrating values and images is described by African-American critic Mary-Helen Washington as "the intimidation of colour."

The cosmetics industry has built solid multi-million dollar businesses on the dominant North American concept that to be loved, to be successful and to validate her own existence, a woman must be beautiful. But, being beautiful, by definition in this context, means to be the blonde-haired, blue-eyed beauty queen, or to be the light-skinned Black woman of the beauty pageants.

Thus, despite feminism's challenging of the beauty industry for setting not only oppressive but also artificial standards of attractiveness, a common female goal among women of all races in multiracial societies is to approximate, as closely as possible, blonde-haired, blue-eyed, long-legged, full-chested, narrow-hipped, "perfection." And this quest, for many, assumes the aspect of a quest for a Holy Grail, even at the price of unnecessary plastic surgery, self-starvation, self-induced vomiting, and diet-pill addiction. These are some of the numerous financially and emotionally costly pathways to beauty, to the myth of True Love and Desirability, which lead ultimately to self-rejection, self-hatred and ultimately a lack of self-esteem.

This self-rejection is multiplied a million times when those very specific physical features that define the Black woman's unique, ethnic reality and basic identity are not in sync with the dominant concept or values about beauty. For many Black women, the most painful forms of rejection have come from within their own racial group. Intra-racial prejudice faults them for their dark skin, full lips, rounded hips, and kinky or curly hair—the very traits inherent in their racial heritage, and symbolic of their ethnic identity.

In confronting the tyranny of beauty, or the "intimidation of colour," Black women are again called upon to find within themselves the psychic capacity to transcend purely physical criteria, barriers, and images in order to redefine "beauty" in their own terms, in their own images, so as to validate their femininity and liberate their sense of personhood and of self-worth. The search for a Black identity and for a way to renew our spirits demands that we too as Black women must wrench from all societies more expansive definitions of beauty and self-worth that include us. The Black Is Beautiful movement has made inroads in this area, but as we are all creatures of our environment, creating new definitions of beauty will be no small task.

Survivors

In discussing this ongoing dilemma we need to develop new paradigms of analysis especially within the women's movement. We need to realize that in white societies the images, struggles, stories, and conditions of Black women can be seen as a fundamental metaphor or paradigm for the stories and conditions of all oppressed women. While gender and race may visibly identify Black women as products, victims, and symbols of oppressive histories, there is another, positive side to their reality.

In the survival of such sexually and racially oppressed women, all women can see the proof of the transcendental power of the human spirit—the real proof of the universal human potential to survive, the real expression of the life-force principle innate in us all.

The very existence of Black women in white societies reminds us that humanity is marked predominantly by our capacity to survive. And from this basic fact of survival, society can learn a timeless principle. As Alice Walker's semi-literate, sexually and economically oppressed child-woman/child-mother heroine, Celie, put it in the 1982 bestseller, *The Color Purple,* "I'm pore, I'm black, I may be ugly....But I'm here."

Day by day Black women have to keep reminding Canadian society that they are here, and that they have every right to be here and to participate fully in the political, economic, and social spheres of society. Hopelessness could easily become the texture of the lives of many Black women. This, however, is not the essential tempo of our lives and our aspirations. No matter what the hardships, our culture is a celebration of life based on the hope for a better life. For without hope we would not have survived the ravages of colonial history. Such hope is what is needed to shift into a new path of consciousness.

Of course, growth in consciousness is difficult, often painful. But if we Black women are to grow beyond our divisiveness, our alienation from ourselves, from each other, and from our very environment, a shift in consciousness is needed. We must move from the power paradigms based on exploitation to paradigms based on cooperation for mutual benefit, and respect for ourselves, for each other, and for our world. Nothing short of a revolution of consciousness is needed—a revolution that begins in our hearts and minds as individuals united for a common cause. The challenge is for all Black women to find and establish the common ground that is needed to move us into the 21st century.

---

[1] A person descended from fugitive slaves belonging to Surinam and the West Indies.

Danisa E. Baloyi

Apartheid and Identity:
Black Women in South Africa

i come to claim my blood ties
— Amina Baraka from
"Soweto Song"

Dr. Danisa E. Baloyi is Executive Director of the National Black Business Caucus in South Africa. She is a member of the US/SA and Danish/SA Business Development Council, and a board member and trustee of companies and trusts including the SA Enterprise Trust. She has worked as a consultant in business development for several organizations including the United Nations Development Fund for Women (UNIFEM), the African-American Institute and the African National Congress.

"Our lives reflect our status under and survival during apartheid rule. Our lives reflect the influence of African tradition, cultural norms, and values. To have our voices heard, our lives must not only be documented by researchers but resound within the Black community in order to empower our people." – Danisa E. Baloyi

The plight of Black South Africans has been amply documented. As a student doing research in the United States, I was amazed by the amount of information on Black South African women, and shocked that only a minuscule amount was actually written by Black women themselves.

We, Black South African women, have to document our situation based on our own experiences and written from our points of view. When testimony about the suffering of Black South African women is gathered by people outside the community, by people who do not share our common suffering, the research actually reveals little about us and more about scholars, their attitudes and perceptions. It lacks depth and feeling.

As Black South African women, we live many lives. Our lives reflect our status under and survival during apartheid rule. Our lives reflect the influence of African tradition, cultural norms, and values. To have our voices heard, our lives must not only be documented by researchers but resound within the Black community in order to empower our people.

Pre-Elections
On April 27, 1994, South Africa came out from under the yoke of statutory apartheid. Under white rule, Black South African women were born and died second-class citizens. Regardless of whether they were professional and educated, statutorily all Black women were regarded as inferiors. We were considered minors; we had no rights. This situation made it very difficult for us to challenge cases of discrimination in legal institutions. We had no legal recourse for acts of brutal discrimination and abuse, within and outside of our environment because male relatives were our legal representatives by law. This translated to no representation should there be a case of domestic violence against women.

To the average Black woman in the South African township or rural area, the new dispensation augurs hope but the despair in their everyday lives seems to signal minimal enthusiasm. The lives of Black women in South Africa are characterized by triple or sometimes quadruple discrimination of race, class, gender and culture/language. South Africa has 11 official languages; some spoken by large and some by small groups who were separated by law during the apartheid era. It is significant that the larger groups looked down upon the smaller groups and in turn practised their own "apartheid" in terms of cultural dominance. The government buttressed this apartheid by separating these groups according to language in homelands in rural areas and townships in urban areas. The people were, therefore, separate and very unequal. The hostilities emanating from these separations brewed undercurrents of dislike among the groups, and sometimes shifted their focus away from the real perpetrators, the apartheid rulers, who engendered the culture of divide and rule. This applied to all Black South Africans, male or female, and laid the ground for inequality.

Women, however, were regarded as inferior regardless of whether they were professionals or were educated. They had no rights and few opportunities. For example, in the central government or the Homelands/ Public sector, there were virtually no women cabinet ministers or women holding senior positions in civil services. Women were relegated to menial positions such as secretaries or clerks.

There were no women superintendents of hospitals and clinics. Virtually all heads of these institutions were male (and still are). There were no women heads of universities, and almost no women principals of high schools. The women principals one found were in lower primary schools. As doctors and nurses, women were always junior to their male counterparts. In all these instances, Black women earned less than their white male or female counterparts and Black male counterparts, even when their qualifications and service were equal.

In business and the private sector, Black women were almost invisible. The companies had either very few or no Black women in significant management positions and they earned relatively lower salaries than their male counterparts and white female counterparts. They were overlooked regardless of their qualifications and most had to work under bosses less qualified. In these cases the women could not advance any legal debate or action since their status was that of minors. In terms of women owning their own businesses, they had to have a male in their family represent them at a financial institution since they had no legal right to represent themselves. Historically, Black people in South Africa have been denied access to capital and had statutory barriers preventing them from doing business properly. For Black women it meant an added burden of having the status of a minor which meant they could not legally apply for a business or a loan. The result was that they had to do business informally and therefore "illegally" and were therefore victims of harassment from the authorities. Their lives were relegated to those of criminals operating outside the law.

Post-Elections

The plight of Black women in South Africa has not changed because of a new government, a new flag and a new President. However, there are positive signs of change that sound a hopeful bell to most Black women.

The advance of Black people into the new power echelons of South Africa has included a few women trailblazers who are assuming significant positions in the new government. It is a fact that the new cabinet and the parliament of the South African government has more women than any other government in the world today, and a significant number of them are Black women who hold important posts. Ministers of Health, Housing, Public Enterprises, and the Speaker of Parliament are women. But the battle is far from won. There was a proposition by the African National Congress (ANC) that at least 30 per cent of government cabinet ministers and members of parliament be women, but that has yet to be realized. At the national level, major strides are being made, but at a provincial level (there are 9 new provinces) one hardly finds any women ministers or director generals. Most provinces do not have even a woman minister, let alone a Black woman.

The upcoming local elections (in October 1995) might usher in a few women leaders, but there is not much room for optimism since South Africa is still deeply rooted in partriarchy. Most South African women will still vote for male candidates rather than for female candidates. The image of female politicians is still not taken seriously. At a parliamentary level, the women politicians have formed a Women's Caucus to work collectively on empowering women to participate in the political process. This task is not going to be easy since the status of women politicians has to be enhanced to make them significant role models. However, a bold and positive start has been made.

In the business sector, progress is slow and change elusive. The country has a significant number of women who are qualified, yet they find it difficult to get businesses off the ground. This sector still reflects a mix of the old and new South Africa. Black women struggle to make a mark, some are successful but most accept that theirs is a token victory. In most organizations, very few are in leadership positions.

Reflections

Earlier as now, Black South African women lived within the family in the African tradition. In our homes, we are generally treated with respect. In most cases, we are the ones who care for our children, since our husbands almost always work in the cities as migrant labourers and only visit once a year. These clearly defined roles of home and communities, however, are completely altered as soon as we venture outside our communities. This has led to a serious crisis of identity, most clearly seen in the struggles of uneducated women.

Black women without formal education constitute a large proportion of the South African population, and the livelihoods of these women are the most disadvantaged within the nation. They hold menial jobs that pay little or nothing at all and struggle just to feed their families. They have few if any marketable skills. Most are employed as domestic workers—the largest number of employed Black women in South Africa today are in the domestic sector. They are abused, underpaid, and endure the most inhumane working conditions that one can imagine. They care for white children who, having been taught from birth that Black people are inferior, treat them as such, and call them 'girl' however old they might be.

By placing most Black families outside urban areas and forcing men to go to the cities for work, apartheid created the added burden of "single parenthood" for countless women. The number of single mothers who earn their livelihoods through domestic work were forced to constantly juggle their roles and responsibilities according to conflicting expectations—from employers, community and families.

The situation earlier was not significantly different for educated Black women since their legal status was the same as that of their uneducated sisters. Hence, they were paid much less than their equally qualified male counterparts, Black or white. Those who, like me, call themselves "educated," confronted a society that told them that success depends on "acting white" and on turning their backs on much of their Africanness. It is no surprise that most of the young people in South Africa believe that being upwardly mobile is synonymous with forsaking African tradition and "acting white" by shunning their Africanness, which includes the African languages.

The constant role changes that Black women—both educated and not—assume at home and in the workplace puts them in a difficult situation. They have to fit into different worlds at different times. It has been a major struggle for Black women to carve out an identity that is not only acceptable in the multiple environments in which they live, but that is also a source of pride—to be who they are and fit properly in all the worlds in which they live.

Monumental changes have come about for South Africa as a whole and for women in particular, beginning with South Africa's decision to sign the Convention on the Elimination of All Forms of Discrimination Against Women (CEDAW). It is interesting to note that there was much discussion about whether this Convention should take priority over the emancipation of all Black South Africans. And we also wondered to what extent Black women would be able to participate in the emancipation process in light of the fact that CEDAW had been approved by the white, male-dominated government in order to appease its white female constituents before the elections to drum up support during elections.

It was not too long ago that I travelled throughout rural South Africa, and no matter where I went, women were asking about the changes to come in the form of South Africa's first non-racist election. In particular, they wondered whether their aspirations, as women, would be put on the agenda of change for South Africa. Some remain vigilant in making sure that change becomes a reality and is sustained and solidified. We have the advantage of learning from the mistakes and triumphs of others.

Identity and self-perception are crucial issues for Black South African women. During apartheid, women were extremely marginalized in education and research. In education, both formal and informal, most of the women were literally pushed to the back of the class. This has served to perpetuate their second-class status, and engender a feeling of helplessness and in some cases resignation to the hand of fate.

The situation is hardly better in the area of research. Despite the large number of research groups existing around the world, most of them are run and controlled by white people. Very few Black people—women or men—are placed in a strategic position to lead the discourse concerning the future of the South African agenda.

Internationally, even fewer Black South African women are organized around issues pertinent to changing the course of their lives. It may be a new political era in South Africa, but as women, they remain visibly isolated. Efforts are being made to link with international organizations, but a lot of work has to be done at home.

Organizations created to improve the lives of Black South Africans have failed to do so. Most of the non-governmental organizations that are supposed to support development and the empowerment of women are still perpetuating the theme of servitude. A master/servant relationship remains very much entrenched within most of these groups. Even today, most Black people are in service positions, rather than in management. It is a situation that must change. Most Black women who assert themselves are categorized as "too aggressive" and "acting like men" and are consequently ostracized and overlooked.

Perhaps no one more than the "educated" Black women must be especially vigilant and refrain from scorning their African heritage after years of white rule. They need to understand, for example, that organizational skills do not exist only among people who can speak English. If a person speaks only Zulu or Tsonga (a smaller group in South Africa), she is no less of a leader. In the new South Africa, all 11 languages have been created equal.

Conclusion

Like all Black South African women, those of us who are researchers, academics and activists have many roles, many identities. Sometimes it is lonely and disorienting. But if we really care about the empowerment of Black women and men of South Africa, we must persevere. The stakes are high and the expectations unrealistic.

National reconciliation will be possible only with a move away from the politics of paternalism. A mental reorientation, reclaiming our proud African identity and acceptance is particularly needed in order to end the madame/servant mentality that exists between white and Black women. Only when that is recognized and eliminated will true equality and power-sharing come. Black women need to feel a part of the change in all respects, to become meaningful leaders and participants in all decision-making processes. Their white counterparts will need to understand that so many years of oppression cannot be changed by the sudden appearance of the new colours of our flag.

A concerted effort has to be made to bring about genuine change and usher in a new era. The world has to play a part in helping the process, but South African women themselves have to take the lead in carving their destiny.

Sergia Galvan

Power, Racism and Identity

talkin bout a woman
talkin bout what the old world
never thought a woman
could be, or do, or imagine
so amazed
they had to look again
they had to change definitions

— Nubia Kai from
"Harriet Tubman"

Sergia Galvan is a member of the Movement for the Identity of Black Women in the Dominican Republic. She is also the coordinator of the Network of Afro-Caribbean and Afro-Latin American Women founded in 1992. She was one of the principal coordinators of the first meeting of Black Latin American and Caribbean Women held in 1992.

"The very process of arriving at an identity needs to be redefined. It has to be grounded in a multicultural and democratic principle that would acknowledge the existing diversities, turning the process of building identity not into a barrier for Black women, but into a tool for reshaping and enlarging their political ideas and involving them actively in the political mainstream." – Sergia Galvan

It has been an extremely difficult task to discuss the evolution of identity among Black women because there is so little research upon which to base such an exploration. Historically, her status as being subordinate and a target of discrimination has been constantly denied. Academics, influenced by this widespread racist ideology, fail to consider the issue worth exploring. Most women who do have access to an academic and intellectual world where such investigations would take place are not Black and are thus generally unaware of the issue. The result is a lack of accurate indicators about the Black woman's economic, political, social and cultural situation. Racism has limited our access to the research that could chronicle our reality.

Where statistics in some of the Latin American and Caribbean countries do exist, they often fail to take into account the ethnic component of oppression, and therefore they do not reflect the real situation. The denial of this problematic issue among many feminist and women's organizations and social researchers, along with the lack of regional action strategies for Black women, have hampered any meaningful approach to the problem.

The ethnic-identity shaping process itself is a complex issue to untangle. Black women do not see themselves in any political, cultural, ideological, or spiritual representation. And when they are represented in society, they are given fake, stereotyped identities imposed on them by national and regional forces. Black women do not have the social strength and power to challenge those identities.

This imposed identity manifests itself most strongly on a personal level and has profound impact on the way Black women experience their sexuality, perceive their body, relate to the question "who am I?", connect to their self-esteem, their self-hatred, their conflict with the mainstream paradigm, their internal fight with the mirror, and their resulting shattered identity.

Identity-shaping goes beyond skin colour, though historically it began and ended with skin colour. The Black women's identity has to be analyzed in the context of other influences that shape identity, but are most often overlooked. Identity is not a collection of fragments; identity is a unity that goes beyond folklore, dances, rituals, colour, and social phenomena. Identity actually goes beyond the subconscious. It is a path among the complex interrelation of the multiple social, political, ideological and cultural variables interacting in the public, private and intimate spheres.

The very process of arriving at an identity needs to be redefined. It has to be grounded in a multicultural and democratic principle that would acknowledge the existing diversities, turning the process of building identity not into a barrier for Black women, but into a tool for reshaping and enlarging their political ideas and involving them actively in the political mainstream.

A very strong link exists between power and racism. It is the force that keeps the subordination of Black women so unshakeable. Discrimination based on racism is reinforced through the usual mechanisms of power consolidation, such as education, media, church, law, family, etc. Most of the time racism is sanctioned in subtle ways through the class structure, labour market and public policies. These elements have a significantly negative influence on the political and social involvement of the already vulnerable ethnic groups.

The economic and structural adjustment policies in most of the countries in Latin America, instead of supporting participation of Black women in the labour market, actually increase their poverty, marginalization and exploitation. Black women are found in the worst-paid jobs in housework and agriculture, and continue to be among the poorest in society.

In addition, another factor that limits Black women's access to work is their "appearance," which is dictated as acceptable or non-acceptable according to norms set by white aesthetics. It cannot be overemphasized how strongly this concept of beauty negatively affects the self-perception of Black women.

Education is another very important element that shapes identity. The majority of the textbooks in the region show stereotyped images of Black women, and Black women tend to be represented in work positions that are not socially valued. In addition, the African heritage of Black women is not acknowledged, even though it is one of the defining factors that characterize the individual nations.

Public health policies related to women's reproductive rights, particularly the ones related to birth control, are going to be of critical importance to

Black women. The recent massive indiscriminate sterilization campaign in Brazil is an example of the inherent dangers that lie for Black women.

At the regional level, the traffic of women (and girls) is increasing dramatically day by day, especially of Black women. The myths and prejudices surrounding Black women's sexuality are used to promote and support the trafficking of Black females in order to satisfy men's sexual fantasies.

Racism is a historical phenomenon occurring as a result of several variables converging and interacting to reinforce social values. Among these, patriarchy has had a definitive role. Any study on the subject that does not scrutinize the link between gender and ethnicity cannot contribute to a meaningful transformation of the Black woman's situation. It is necessary to move beyond a polarized analysis that asks whether you are first a woman and then Black, or you are first Black and then a woman. This type of approach does not help us in either creating strategies or in the subjective process of shaping an identity.

The Latin American feminist movement has failed to envision a holistic and gender approach to combating racism at both a theoretical and practical level. The big challenge within the movement is to develop an approach that would help to transform the global reality, not just a small portion of it.

The Afrocentric feminism of the North has provided valuable support for ethnic specificity in the Latin American region. It has helped to amplify the transcultural vision of Latin American feminism and propose new categories of analysis. It has allowed Black women in the region to structure the debate and establish theoretical bases to articulate the relationship between gender and ethnicity. More importantly, it has promoted a process of self-discovery and self-realization leading to a positive reaffirmation of Black women.

Since the mid-1980s the Black and indigenous women of Latin America and the Caribbean have taken various initiatives to open up the space within the feminist movement for more reflection and debate on the issue of ethnicity and race. A crucial step was taken in 1992 in organizing the First Encounter of Black Latin American and Caribbean Women in the Dominican Republic. This meeting provided 350 women from 30 countries of the region the opportunity to meet, analyze, strategize, reflect and build alliances around issues of common concern. The issues included identity, racism, violence, health, sexuality, power, international cooperation, feminism and communication. The most important outcome of the meeting was the establishment of the Network of Afro-Caribbean and Afro-Latin American Women.

As a result of these meetings, Black women's issues have received greater visibility. There is a growing awareness and sensibility toward Black women's issues within the women's movement. Black women's demands have also had an impact on different international organizations. The fact that organizations like the United Nations have started to recognize racism as an issue is a direct outcome of our organizing strength.

We know we have to face many more challenges. We need to strengthen our regional and national organizations; we need to establish an information network within the movement; we need to have a greater impact on government; and we need to find common ground within the feminist and social movements. We need to push toward the definition and implementation of public policies that contribute to the transformation of our reality. We need to strengthen our visibilty, and demand that research, analysis, and theoretical work regarding our situation be carried out, as well as ethical approaches be developed. We need to support and interact with organizations that have started to work on women's identities.

Black women's identity problem is a reality that cannot be overlooked. The discourse on diversity and plurality must become part of our agendas. We have to work towards a development model that advances reaffirmation, recognition and respect for ethnic, racial and gender identities. As our work forges ahead, our hope grows.

Peggy Antrobus

Women in the Caribbean: The Quadruple Burden of Gender, Race, Class and Imperialism

I am both *Black* and *a woman…*
And yet I am continually asked
to prioritize my consciousness; is
race more important; is gender
more important? Which is more
severe, etc.? The fallacy lies not in
struggling with the answer, in
trying to figure out which is the
correct answer for the group at
hand, but the fallacy lies with
the question itself.

— Patricia Hill Collins

Peggy Antrobus is coordinator of the Women and Development (WAND) Unit at the University of the West Indies and general co-ordinator of DAWN (Development Alternatives with Women for a New Era). Antrobus has a background in economics, social work, community development and administration and was the former director of the Jamaican Women's Bureau.

"It is difficult to separate the issues of race, class, gender, nationality and imperialism, and it is important to see the link between all forms of oppression, rather than singling out one as the primary factor." – Peggy Antrobus

I work at several levels. I head the Women and Development (WAND) Unit at the regional University of the West Indies which works at national and local levels to strengthen the participation of women in the socio-economic development of the English-speaking Caribbean. I also coordinate a network of women from the economic South promoting Development Alternatives with Women for a New Era (DAWN). The connection between these activities has enabled me to understand how global trends, played out through policies at the national level, affect the lives of women living in local communities. The connections also illustrate how the persistence of the legacy of colonialism with its racial/ethnic, sexist and class biases has resulted in a system of "global, gendered apartheid"—a global economic system characterized by the exploitation of the labour of women of colour everywhere.

Although in countries with Black populations, factors other than race play a significant part in the securing of livelihood, it is nevertheless true that, with few exceptions, the countries themselves suffer the effect of globalized apartheid (one only has to think of many of the countries in Africa today!). It is difficult to separate the issues of race, class, gender, nationality and imperialism, and it is important to see the link between all forms of oppression, rather than singling out one as the primary factor.

The Caribbean society today, which reflects our history of colonialism, remains deeply stratified along class and racial lines, with Black people representing the majority of the poor. As a result of slavery of the Africans and indentured labour of the Asians, agricultural labour was associated with the hardest conditions and the lowest returns. With the best lands controlled by a few European plantation owners, the Black population of small farmers was driven to work on the most marginal lands, without capital or technology. The rural small farmers thus inherited a legacy of persistent poverty and deprivation, which is still with them. Hundreds of years after emancipation, the small farmers continue to be overwhelmingly poor, and it is not difficult to understand why very few young people today wish to follow their parents into agriculture. It is ironic because the countries in the Caribbean are still largely agricultural societies. Between 30 to 40 per cent of the small farmers are women, and they suffer the triple burden of being poor, female and living in rural areas.

Women's poverty has its foundation in the fact that much of the work of women in the household, in subsistence agriculture and in the community is either unwaged or poorly paid for. While middle-income women are able to compensate to some extent for their unwaged housework through marriage to well-paid men and/or through their own higher wage or salary, working-class women have no such opportunities. Thus the large amount of unwaged work that working-class or poor women do condemns them to a cycle of poverty, be it in rural or urban areas. One cannot understand poverty and exploitation without considering the impact of women's unwaged work on the economic system.

The majority of the poor are women. While many of them have large families, they are not poor *because* they have many children. In fact, the reverse is true. They may have many children because they are poor, which means they have very limited options in terms of education, training and employment, and see children as a source of wealth, perhaps the only source of affirmation. For many, the cycle starts with early motherhood, while they are still at school. With the failure of the baby's father to support their child, the women often turn for support to other men, who leave her with yet more children. And so the cycle is repeated. Serial mating in the Caribbean has to be seen as a survival strategy. We have to thus consider women's poverty in the context of massive unemployment and the inability of many men to support their children.

In addition, securing a livelihood in the rural areas of the Caribbean often means living with a minimum of services such as electricity, a reliable water supply, transportation, shops, clinics, schools, housing, etc. Many rural women have to walk great distances to reach their small plot of land, which is often on a hillside and thus difficult to access as well as environmentally and economically precarious.

The struggle to secure a livelihood for many women in the Caribbean is almost impossible to convey. The employment options available for those who escape into the urban areas are few. In urban areas many women engage in domestic work and petty trading, with prostitution a last, but always available, resort. All are survival strategies. In any event, their living conditions and their earnings are hardly any better when compared to those they left behind in the rural villages.

Migration to other countries in search of work is also a common survival strategy for Caribbean women. When they migrate, Caribbean women remain in close communication with their families in the Caribbean, sending regular remittances to support elderly parents and children; sometimes sending children back into the care of elderly parents.

Into this situation of persistent poverty and deprivation, dependency and marginalization for the majority of people, has come the macroeconomic policies of structural adjustment adopted by many Caribbean governments in the 1980s. These policies have certainly served to exacerbate an already bad situation.

Introduced to alleviate the debt crisis of the 1980s, the structural adjustment policies have come to be associated with cuts in public services and subsidies to basic goods (food and fuel); increases in the price of transportation, housing, water, electricity and drugs; privatization of government assets; and trade liberalization and devaluation of the currency. The consequences of these policies have been devastating. They have led to increasing unemployment, poverty, social disintegration and violence. The poor have suffered the most—and women, children and the elderly within that social group more than anyone else. Because of the additional role that women play in taking care of the sick, the elderly and the children, women of all classes have especially borne the impact of the deterioration in the quality of people's lives.

Policies of structural adjustment are deeply gendered, based as they are on an assumption that justifies exploitation of women's time and labour—both in the household and in the workplace. For at the centre of these policies are those intended to reduce consumption (e.g., cuts in government expenditures on social services, which both jeopardize jobs in sectors in which women predominate and assume that women will fill the gaps created by these cuts) and those aimed at increasing production (based on assumptions about a ready supply of cheap female labour).

When governments privatize social services, the poor cannot access these services and have to depend on the services of women in their own households. These services are not remunerated, so governments save money at the expense of women's unwaged labour in their households.

But women's waged labour is also exploited in the context of these policies. On the production side, the promotion of export-oriented industries depends on cheap female labour. In global terms, one finds that these industries are moving into countries where there are large and vulnerable supplies of cheap labour—and that the labour-force is overwhelmingly female. The multinational corporations that come to invest in our countries are not locating here because they want to create employment. Rather, they are coming because they want to maximize their profits. In that way they are taking full advantage of women who are poor and desperately need money for the support of their children and families.

Our governments facilitate these arrangements, seeing them as short-term solutions to chronic unemployment. In fact, these factories come to our countries under government sponsorship and at considerable costs to the tax-payers of the country in terms of loans for infrastructure, foregone taxes and public-sector time, and most importantly, at the expense of alternative projects and strategies for solving historic problems of persistent poverty, unemployment and dependency.

Part of the deal in the promotion of export-processing zones is that labour cannot be unionized. In many of our countries the local labour unions accept these restrictions, and one might wonder whether they would do so if the workforce were not overwhelmingly female.

In short, at the centre of these policies of structural adjustment is the devaluation of women's work in the household as well as in the labour force.

These policies are not peculiar to the Caribbean; they are part of a process of the globalization of economies through the introduction of neo-liberal economic policies, a process accelerated by the collapse of the socialist economies of Eastern Europe. This is where the work of DAWN complements my work with rural women in the Caribbean.

One of DAWN's current projects is a critique of the current global economic system and a proposal of Alternative Economic Frameworks.[1] Within this analysis, DAWN will be investigating the way in which women secure a livelihood; critiquing the dominant paradigm; and making recommendations regarding what needs to happen if people are to survive into the next century. In this context, we have to pay more attention to the survival strategies of Black women. It means going back to our roots, to our identity as Black women, to the values which have enabled us to survive, with dignity and hope, the devastation of slavery and exploitation. It means going back to the strategies for collective survival—to the priority given to the well-being of our children, to respect and care of our elders, to cooperation with each other, and to the conservation of the natural resource base. Cultural identity can be of critical importance if we are going to survive in a global, disembodied marketplace whose values are opposed to everything we hold dear, and where profits for the few take priority over secure livelihoods for the many.

In a global economic system where size becomes a factor for competitiveness, the island-states of the Caribbean are at a distinct disadvantage. Our survival cannot therefore depend on "being competitive." We must assert other values, the values of our identity as a community of Black women.

As we face the ongoing crises generated by the globalization of our economies, the time has come for us to try, following in the footsteps of Marcus Garvey, to make links between Black communities, including those in the diaspora. The time has come for us to try to form some kind of political movement to assert our values for the survival and liberation of Black people everywhere.

[1] DAWN's other projects focus on the environment and on reproductive rights and population.

Felicia Ekejiuba

Gender-responsive Agenda for Equitable Development

Another empowering act has been to take charge of defining my group, of naming myself. Naming oneself, defining oneself and thereby taking the power to define out of the hands of those who wield that power over to you, is an important act of empowerment....The act of self-definition thus makes clear our worth and entitlement, and sets forth our view of ourselves as one which will have to be reckoned with.

— Judy Scales-Trent

Formerly a Professor of Anthropology at the University of Nigeria at Nsukka, Felicia Ekejiuba has also taught at a number of universities in the U.S. Her most recent work has been "Participatory and Sustainable Research with Rural Women." She is currently the Regional Programme Advisor for UNIFEM in Nigeria.

"The hearthold-household distinction is intrinsic to research and project designs in relation to decision-making, risk taking, resource and information sharing, and responses to new initiatives. It enables us to see women not as appendages to the household but as active, often independent actors." – Felicia Ekejiuba

Women in general and Black women in particular constantly have to deal with the related psychological and economic issues of identity and livelihood as a result of their structural position in society. In Africa, whatever their marital status, women have initiated development efforts and participated actively in social and economic processes in their communities. This paper attempts to link the two social concepts of hearthold and household, and thus focus on the existing realities of many West African societies.[1]

Rethinking "Household"

Researchers have long used the household as an instrument for collecting data and analyzing many gender issues. But how useful and accurate has it been to rely on a unit of analysis that ignores the true nature and identity of Black women in African societies?

Currently, the definition of the "household" consists of the father, mother(s), and children, with the man as the head and *sole provider*. Using data based on this definition of the household, state and national policies are designed to create programmes essential for maintaining the household (e.g., wage structure, tax policies, etc.). Yet these are also the policies that allow the head of the household to collect allowances for the wife and children, while denying these rights to women.

To increase the visibility of women through development planning, especially in non-Western capitalist societies such as those in Africa, the very concept of household needs rethinking. The conceptual and practical problems posed by using the household as a unit for designing projects in Africa have been amply documented.[2] Rather than belonging to a household as defined by researchers, individuals actually belong to a network of households. The network is determined by the kind of goods and services required, as many households depend on transfers of goods and services from others for their livelihood.[3] Such studies have therefore demonstrated the need for a more systematic analysis of intra- and inter-household dynamics.[4]

Since development processes should be geared towards improving living standards and quality of life for all, data that looks more carefully at women's economic and social contributions enables us to monitor whose life is being improved and at whose expense.

The Hearthold: A Female-Centred Unit

The search for improved data for participatory, equitable development should therefore re-focus on the autonomy and interdependence of gender. This also means that we should focus more attention on the unit referred to by the development and anthropological literature as the "small household"[5] or "female-headed household." These units, sometimes independent but often a subset of the household, are invariably headed and controlled by women. However, the autonomy enjoyed by such units have largely been unrecognized. In most cases, they have been ignored in the process of data generation and analysis as well as in the process of policy-making and resource allocation.

The search for a more gender-sensitive and equitable framework for development and resource allocation should focus much more on the female-headed unit. This unit is defined here as the "hearthold."[6] It can either have an independent existence or be nestled in the household, in which case it is like an extension of the intimate mother-child bond. Centred on the hearth, or stove (in an African vernacular, *ekwu, mkpuke*), this unit is demographically made up of a woman and all dependents, which include her children and her co-resident relatives and non-relatives. These co-residents assist her permanently or temporarily in providing food, caring for and nurturing members of her hearthold who share in the food cooked on her hearth for a significant part of their life. The male spouse is either fully a member of this hearthold or, most commonly, oscillates between several hearcholds—those of his wives, mother and mistresses.

The hearthold is thus primarily a unit of consumption, but is also a unit of production. As a reproductive and socializing unit, it depends on other hearcholds and households, and as a consequence members may move temporarily from one unit to another.

Even when there is only one hearthold in the household, a pattern of interaction and reciprocal exchange exists between the head of household (male) and head of the hearthold (female). Both male and female heads have a distinct set of dependents and clearly defined responsibilities. These factors are essential to our understanding of intra-household autonomy and inter-dependence, which results in different patterns of production, investment, and response to initiatives. The different ways the hearthold is linked to larger units (other households, their component heartholds, and the community) for access to labour—through the informal work groups or hiring of labour—and other resources is also relevant for understanding the diversified production strategies and the differential impact of development planning on the sexes.

In different parts of Africa, rural and urban, among educated and uneducated alike, a number of situations give rise to these female-focused heartholds. These include polygyny, or the multiple-spouse marriage system, prevalent among Moslems, some urban-based educated groups, and among many farming communities, particularly the slash-and-burn type. Other situations include: leviratic unions, in which a man takes over the social responsibility of protection and care of his deceased brother's wife (or wives) in addition to being responsible for his own wife (or wives); woman-to-woman marriage;[7] three or more generational "households" of parents and their married children;[8] joint family household of brothers in a patrilineal system or of sisters in a matrilineal system or of brother(s) and their unwed/divorced sister(s) in a patrilineal system; divorce, migration or death-induced absence of males in any of the above.

The household in all instances has common resources—land, cattle, fish pond, fruit trees—which are controlled and managed by the household head but which he subdivides among the hearthold heads as a source of income. Each hearthold is often though not necessarily co-resident, so it owns its own space (a house, flat, room); it has its own water storage facilities, cooking utensils, cooking fuel, yam or grain storage facilities, traction engine or farm animals, and land. Each hearthold head is primarily responsible for providing members of her hearthold with food; clothing; school fees; and care of children, the elderly and the sick members of the hearthold. She may be a farmer, trader, craftswoman, wage earner, a professional in the formal sector, or she may be a combination of these. In search of additional sources of income, a woman may migrate to cities or other countries in order to meet her various obligations both to her hearthold and to her kin and community.

The male head of household, even in a monogamous family situation, often controls his own finances, barn, land, labourers, etc., and contributes to, but is never solely responsible for, the total expenditure of the hearthold(s). Where several heartholds form subsets of the household (e.g., in a polygamous marriage situation), he contributes to all the heartholds. In return, he retains his membership in the hearthold and his position as the household head, which entitles him to periodic but guaranteed access to food, labour and sexual services from the hearthold heads. His primary responsibilities to each hearthold are to provide a dwelling unit and to assure each access to resources such as land, cattle and fruit trees. He also supplements school fees and hospital bills of hearthold members and is expected to provide meat for each of the units. In recent times, however, high commodity prices, low stagnant incomes, unemployment, forced retirement and retrenchment of workers and repeated devaluation of currencies have dramatically reduced or eliminated the expected contributions of household heads. Correspondingly, it has added greater pressures on the hearthold heads to earn more from farming, trading and other informal/formal sector earnings.

Gender-sensitive data should focus on the dynamics of the relationship between the household and the heartholds in order to facilitate planning and mainstreaming of women's issues in ways that will improve women's lives. Data should consider the role of hearthold heads as they strive to protect their autonomy and financial independence while cooperating with the household head in order to ensure access to production factors and the survival of the total unit.

The complex interplay of cooperation and conflict across household and hearthold boundaries in pooling labour for childcare, production, processing, and distribution of agricultural products are also part of the gender-sensitive data that are needed for farming-systems research and other participatory, action-oriented programmes. To ensure food security, development agents have to re-focus on understanding the gender ideology and division of labour within the hearthold. Women's resource needs are often masked when we focus only on the household in development and national policies.

An analysis of the interaction between the household and the hearthold clearly demonstrates women's reality: women's labour and access to land are critical factors for social reproduction; household and hearthold heads do not always pool resources; women are constantly balancing their time and labour between production for the hearthold and the household; sources of earning a livelihood are dwindling for women; and withdrawal of women's access to and control over production resources increases gender inequality, impoverishes women, and, above all, threatens food security and self-sufficiency of the hearthold, of the community, and of the nation. In addition, in spite of the increasing need for access to land for food production by hearthold heads, the household head can and has been known to sell or pawn land to raise the capital to marry more wives, purchase radios, engage in betting, build a house or take chieftaincy and other titles to enhance his prestige. These patterns of intra-household relationships are often overlooked when the focus is on the household alone or on the individual adult male and female in their household. Yet the structure and nature of household-hearthold interactions are relevant to development processes that introduce new technology, capital, credit or additional possibilities for income-generation.

The hearthold-household distinction is intrinsic to research and project designs in relation to decision-making, risk taking, resource and information sharing and responses to new initiatives. It enables us to see women not as appendages to the household but as active, often independent actors. Women are concerned with increasing their options and with the impact of these choices on their dependents. Data separated out by gender therefore needs to focus more on the multiple goals and responsibilities, and the diverse sources of income. Attention must be paid to daily and seasonal routines of hearthold and household members, as well as to accumulation and investment by gender rather than by household time allocations.

The exchanges, linkages and patterns of interaction between heartholds and households are far too important to be relegated to footnotes and caveats. They should be incorporated into the analytical framework[9] as we address and mainstream women's concerns, responsibilities, and goals, and as we strive to provide women with increased access to development resources by using a female-centred unit, here defined as the hearthold, in sampling, data generation, analysis, resource sharing and planning.

Households, Heartholds and a Development Project

The distinction between the hearthold and household was particularly useful in carrying out socio-economic surveys and sensitization in 77 rural villages in Nigeria for a rural water project. Prior to implementing the project, an assessment was made of the priority which the villages attached to having safe, pipe-borne, potable water over other needs such as rural electrification. The willingness, readiness and ability of the villagers to contribute to the operational maintenance of the water was assessed once the technocrats had installed the pipes. Several aspects of the goals of the survey and the project made it imperative to focus on the hearthold as a unit of data generation and analysis.

Women and children have the responsibility of fetching water, often from distances ranging from two to eight kilometres. Women's need for water—for cooking, cleaning, laundering, bathing (self and children) and drinking—differs from that of the men, who need water mainly for bathing and drinking. Each hearthold owned its own containers for storing water and only the more affluent in the communities could purchase, through either collective contributions of both hearthold and household heads, water containers built of galvanized iron sheets able to hold up to 1,000 gallons of water. Women were responsible for ensuring that water was clean and safe, by boiling or adding alum. It was only the women who could effectively monitor the increase or reduction of water-borne diseases, such as diarrhoea. The instrument for the survey therefore had entries that distinguished income, education and water use of the household from that of the hearthold heads. There were significant differences in the priority placed on water. Whereas many women listed water and health centres as top priorities, men mentioned roads, community banks and electricity as being more important than water. The women were happy that their opinion was sought on this occasion. As one woman said, "People in the past treated us as if we did not exist, as if our opinions were not necessary. So we ignored the team and later there was nobody to keep the pipe-borne water clean, that is, if there was any water from the tap."

In response to a questionnaire, more women than men were prepared to contribute money and labour to keep the pipe-borne water clean. Some women were prepared to serve on the village water committee and a few were prepared to undergo the training necessary to maintain the water pumps so as to prevent stalemates in the event that pumps break down.

Field experiences such as this one make it clear that the hearthold, not the household, is a more basic and more clearly defined unit of representation. The household is, in fact, a convergence of separate economies. It is also a convergence of individuals with varying access to resources and with different goals and responsibilities.

These facts are often ignored in most development planning and policy making, resulting in negative consequences for women. For women to be equal partners in development, it is necessary that we see them at the centre of activities, in the hearthold, instead of at the margins of the household.

Women have always been fully involved in the mainstream of indigenous economic activities. Their continued involvement in all stages of planned intervention will not only empower them but also assure their active participation in sustainable and equitable development.

1 This paper was first presented at a workshop on "Reconceptualizing the Household" sponsored by the Social Science Research Council, Cambridge, Massachusetts in 1984.

2 See Guyer, J. 1986; Guyer, J. and Peters, P. 1986; and Elwert, G. 1984.

3 Wong, D. 1984.

4 Guyer, J. 1986, 95; Peters, P. 1986; Jones, C.W. 1986, 113.

5 Elwert, G. 1984.

6 Ekejiuba, F. 1984.

7 Amadiume, I. 1987.

8 Hill, P. 1967.

9 Peters, P. 1986, 137.

8

Andrée Nicola McLaughlin

The Impact of the Black Consciousness and Women's Movements on Black Women's Identity: Intercontinental Empowerment

I've come this far to freedom and
I won't turn back.
I'm climbing to the highway
from my old dirt track
  I'm coming and I'm going,
  And I'm stretching
  and I'm growing
And I'll reap what I've been
sowing or my skin's not black.
                — *Naomi Long Madgett*
                      from "Midway"

Dr. Andrée Nicola McLaughlin is founding international coordinator of the International Cross-Cultural Black Women's Studies Summer Institute headquartered in London and New York. Professor of Literature and Language and of Interdisciplinary Studies at Medgar Evers College of the City University of New York, Dr. McLaughlin has written extensively on Black women's identity.

> *"In most instances, Black women seek empower-*
> *ment through both types of political organizing: as*
> *members of their cultural groups and as women."*
> *– Andrée Nicola McLaughlin*

The Geledés Black Women's Institute (Brazil) • The Group of Kanak and Exploited Women in Struggle (Kanaky, also known as New Caledonia) • The Centre of Study & Research for the Development of Afro-Colombian Women • The Association of Women's Clubs (Zimbabwe) • The Congress of Black Women of Canada • The Black Women's Identity Movement (the Dominican Republic) • The Movement for Defense of Black Women's Rights (France) • (The Dalit) Women's Organization for Liberation & Development (India) • The Caribbean Association for Feminist Research and Action (Trinidad & Tobago) • The Cross-Cultural Initiative of Black Women in Germany • The Black Women's Union of Venezuela • The National Black Women's Health Project (the United States of America) • Women's Action for Development (Uganda) • Akina Mama wa Africa (the United Kingdom) • The Black Women's Collective (Panama) • The Black Women's Group (Australia)

T he proliferation of Black women's organizations in the last decade signals a global phenomenon. Such organized political activity on the part of self-identified "Black women" reflects a burgeoning, intercontinental Black women's consciousness movement.[1] Represented in numerous local, national and regional initiatives for Black women's empowerment, this movement gave rise to the International Cross-Cultural Black Women's Studies Summer Institute in 1987. An autonomous, voluntary intercontinental network of Black women, the Institute has held five annual forums, and now convenes biannually, to address global issues of concern: peace; human, national and democratic rights; and economic development. The network spans Africa, Asia, the Americas, Europe and the Pacific, and includes:

    • Women who, at the invitation of women's organizations, have travelled to Britain, the United States, Zimbabwe, Aotearoa (New Zealand), Germany or Venezuela for the purpose of learning first-hand of women's plights.

• Women who are poised to develop action strategies for one or more global issue such as "Women's Condition," "Women and Communications," "Women and the Politics of Food," "Human Rights & Indigenous Peoples in the Information Age," "Black People in the European Community," and "The Black Woman's Five Centuries of Resistance and Cultural Affirmation in the Americas."

• Women who believe that in efforts to change our societies and the world, we as exploited people and as women, have been marginalized by racism, sexism, and economic class bias, elitism, or sectarianism on the part of state, reactionary and progressive forces.

• Women who feel confident that we in particular, and women of exploited and oppressed nations and peoples in general, can make a positive difference in the quality of our own lives and toward the well-being of humanity.

• Women who appreciate that we have the capacity to create enduring and globally-responsible economic, political, social and cultural structures that enable us to determine our destinies.

• Women who share common historical experiences and recognize the need to mobilize across national boundaries to restore the integrity of Black women's lives and cultures.

The intercontinental Black women's consciousness movement has its roots in the post-World War II era of national independence and liberation movements in Africa, Asia, Latin America and the Pacific. Black women did play, and continue to play, key roles in these anti-colonial, anti-imperialist movements. Zimbabwean scholar Rudo Gaidzanwa's explanation for why women of the Southern Africa region became active in national liberation struggles has global application: "Most threw their weight behind the anti-colonial forces on the understanding that they were more likely to realize their interests in a non-colonial system."[2]

Susanna Ounei, an indigenous activist, acknowledges that her involvement in the struggle for the independence of the French colony of Kanaky (a non-self-governing Pacific territory known as New Caledonia) stems from her experiences as a child: "At the convent school I attended, the white kids got all the attention, while we Kanak kids were called 'dirty Kanaks' even by white teachers."[3] These insults upset her, and she recalls thinking when she was only 12 that "one day a Black movement would be formed to struggle against these injustices."[4]

That day of Black resistance materialized for Ounei when, in 1969, a son of a Kanak chief returned from study and activism in France, bringing with him the fervour of Black nationalism. She remembers how he formed the Foulards Rouges, "initially...a movement to promote Kanak culture and to combat racism."[5] Ounei, along with many other Melanesian nationals, joined this incipient movement, proudly proclaiming their Kanak cultural identity. Unequivocally, she contends, "it paved the way for other grassroots groups to call for the return of the land taken by the French (in 1853) and for independence from France."[6]

While the Kanak struggle developed into an independence movement, it had begun as one to end racial injustice. Black nationalist movements against white domination at first emphasized racial equality, since race was used "as a basis for differentiating access...to health, education, jobs and land."[7] Seeking to redefine and empower ourselves in our respective national contexts, Black people have continued direct, political challenges to the status quo. The ramifications of such mass resistance—in Kanaky, Trinidad & Tobago, Great Britain, South Africa, Brazil, India, the United States and in many other countries—have been manifold.

The global, political reawakening of Black people in the second half of the twentieth century has brought issues of identity, language and culture to the fore. Eva Johnson, Aboriginal playwright, explains the evolution of Black self-identification for indigenous people in Australia: "The half-caste situation came during colonization, as the frontier was being won by all the white men. It was part of the genocide and part of the process of the invasion, raping the women as they went along."[8] While Aboriginal people have put to rest their use of terms like "half-caste," white people still employ them: "They say, 'She's not real Aboriginal because she's a half-caste,'" Johnson maintains. "[Whites] use the term to discredit us whereas before they used the terms half-caste and quarter-caste to make *themselves* feel better about us *not* being Aboriginal. The more white you were, the better you were accepted into white society."[9]

Today, Johnson comfortably asserts, "But now I claim my Blackness and I say, 'I am Black.' And of course all Aboriginal people do identify as being Black now—this is what's making us stronger."[10] She is confident that her people "are becoming more positively identified with our colour, our origin, our indigenousness, [our] Aboriginality."[11]

Johnson traces the origins of Black consciousness among Aborigines to the Black Power and the United States' Black Panther movements. Beginning in 1967, "all Aboriginal kids started walking around with 'Black Is Beautiful' T-shirts. And in the late 60s and 70s, Afro hairstyles were in and everyone wanted an Afro hairstyle."[12] An outgrowth of this cultural reassertion was the demand for social justice: "It was in 1972 that the first land rights movement started," states Johnson. "We set up an Aboriginal embassy."[13]

The Black consciousness movement that originated in the mid-1960s as a push for Black empowerment remains ongoing and dynamic, underscoring new self-identifications that Black women have assumed in many places around the world. Katharina Oguntoye, co-editor of the first book by Black German women, *Afro-German Women: Showing Our Colours* (1986), distinguishes between the terms Afro-German and Black German: "In the first instance, (it) refers to our heritage, not to the colour of our skin."[14] Collectively, Black Germans include those of African or Asian parentage and most have an African or African-American parent and a German parent.

Oguntoye attributes the introduction of Black consciousness in Germany to the late Audre Lorde, renowned African-American poet and author, who lectured extensively in Germany during 1984 and encouraged Black Germans to tell their stories in print. A subsequent documentary film has had a profound impact on Black Germans nationally, the majority of whom have grown up in a predominantly white society. Oguntoye recounts:

> In 1986, our book was issued and the first Afro-German groups began to have their meetings. It was a great experience for all of us. After two years, there were many Black German groups all over the country under the umbrella of Initiative of Black Germans....In 1988, a Black German group was formed in East Berlin.[15]

The national organizing efforts of the Initiative of Black Germans has put them in contact "with Afro-Dutch and Afro-British people. We know some Afro-Swedish and one Afro-Russian," shares Oguntoye. "In my family, there are Afro-Czechoslovakians."[16]

As the weak national response to recent, highly publicized racist violence by neo-Nazis suggests, many white Germans still deny the Black presence and the existence of racism in Germany. Oguntoye comments that white Germans "don't want to remember the Nazi period and German colonialism, which introduced Black people, in significant numbers, to their society."[17] Given this circumstance, one main focus of Black groups is developing their "identity as multicultural and as Black people." In the Initiative of Black Germans, according to Oguntoye, "we wish deeply not to be separated and to stand together whether we are African, African-German, or Asian-

German."[18] A subsequent focus of Black organizing has been to increase their visibility to resist racist violence.

These personal testimonies of Black women in Kanaky, Australia and Germany confirm that Black identity has been adopted in a variety of ways by exploited or oppressed peoples for national, democratic and human rights; and for social, economic and political power. The diversity of Black identity mirrors the range of historical circumstances and priorities of different groups.

For Black women of South Africa, Black political-class identification has been a crucial dimension of the struggle for a democratic society, encompassing Africans, Asians and so-called coloureds, that is, people of mixed-race backgrounds.[19] Together, these groups have comprised the critical mass of opposition to colonial apartheid, the legally proscribed domination of Blacks by a white minority (until mid-1993).

In Aotearoa (New Zealand), Black identity has represented a practical alliance among the indigenous Maori, the New Zealand-born Pacific Islanders, and the Pacific Island immigrants who are commonly affected by separate development policies of the state (that are disadvantageous for those who are not white) and, consequently, are relegated to a common social class.[20]

In Britain, Black women include "Africans, continental and of the diaspora, and Asians primarily of Indian subcontinent descent."[21] As one Black woman of Caribbean origin in Britain declares, "When we use the term 'Black,' we use it as a political term. It doesn't describe skin colour; it defines our situation here in Britain. We're here as a result of British imperialism, and our continued oppression in Britain is a result of British racism."[22] For yet another Black woman of Asian background, Afro-Asian unity in Britain stands as "a mark of rising strength and confidence in a bid to break with the divisive ethnic boundaries and evolve common political strategies to face institutionalized racism and right-wing attacks."[23]

In India, Black identity links the estimated 280 million Dalits, or "Black Untouchables," to Black people worldwide who are battling domination. Original inhabitants of India, the Dalits, who share common ancestors with Africans and who resisted and were later enslaved by Aryan invaders, contest the Aryan doctrine of Brahminical superiority and the excruciating exploitation perpetrated by India's caste system.[24]

In the Netherlands, we find that the Black Dutch include immigrants and descendants of peoples from Indonesia, South Africa, Nigeria, Turkey, the

Moluccans, the Caribbean, China and other parts of the world where Black people are aboriginals.[25] Here, Black self-identification is increasingly inclusive of people of Asian, Pacific, African, and even Southern European (e.g., Italian) ancestry.

In Russia, the disintegration of the Soviet Union has spurred the formation of an African-Russian Society of St. Petersburg to combat an overt anti-Black sentiment that has emerged and is most seriously evidenced in the surge of abandoned Black children in orphanages. Yelena Khanga, a Black Russian, informs us that the Black population in the former Union of Soviet Socialist Republics largely consists of the "offspring of mixed marriages between Soviet young men and women and African students."[26] Russian-born Blacks "hope [the new association] will unite all Soviets who have their roots in Africa."[27]

In the United States and Canada, Black identity has long brought together African culture and political class.[28] It links peoples of African descent historically and culturally to both the African continent and the pan-African world community, and politically to all Black-identified peoples opposing supremacist doctrines and the latter's detrimental effects on human existence. In this context, ancestry, that is, African heritage, determines Black identity, and one drop of blood provides sufficient credential for claiming Black culture and embracing Black political class.

The most profound significance of Malcolm X to Black people globally was, perhaps, his articulation of Black identification. He directed us to forge an identity that, on the one hand, entails resistance to oppression and exploitation in conjunction with other people suffering under white rule. On the other hand, in regard to Black people of African descent, Malcolm X inspired our reclamation of African culture and history with his call for "African"- or "Afro"- distinguishing national or regional identifications, mandating a conscious cultural and historical affinity to Africa and the African world. In effect, Malcolm X introduced us to a Black diaspora and broadened awareness of the African diaspora.

In other parts of the Black diaspora, self-definition is primarily associated with nationality, ethnicity, and kinship systems. Black identity, in these instances, commonly refers to the cultural unity of people of African descent.

In Latin America and the Caribbean, issues of Black identity and culture are more complex than they appear. Phenotype, or looking African in terms of skin colour, hair texture, and facial features, invariably determines Black identity in this region. However, more than a few governments (Mexico, Peru, French Guyana, Bolivia, and Argentina, for example) try to keep their

Black populations invisible, usually claiming that Blacks have been biologically and culturally assimilated. Still, in countries such as Cuba and Brazil, African culture defines the national culture and is embraced by Blacks and many whites alike. Nevertheless, because of the prevailing low socio-economic status of Black people in these societies, concerns about who controls and interprets this culture persist.

Politics, culture, and identity are undoubtedly intertwined throughout the Black world. Through the work of the International Cross-Cultural Black Women's Studies Summer Institute, Black women, by consensus, hold that social class, political class, and culture define the global diaspora of Black women. As a social class, Black people are among the world's disfranchised whose plight is characterized by a condition of poverty, violence, misery, and inequality brought on by colonialism and imperialism. As a Black political class, the oppressed—self-defined as Black—act on behalf of the social class to oppose the prevailing socio-economic interests of the dominant group. As a cultural group, Black people, in their distinct geographical and interactive historical contexts, are bound by what the late Frantz Fanon said are "our efforts to describe, justify and praise the action in the sphere of thought through which that people has created itself and keeps itself in existence."[29] It is through our belief systems, customs, arts, technologies, idioms, and so forth that we preserve the culture as self-identified African women, Afro-Caribbean women, Afro-Latin American women, Aboriginal women, Afro-German women, African-American women, and Dalit women.

While there is no homogeneous Black identity, as this applies to geography, phenotype, culture, or ideology, the threatened survival of our cultural groups moves Black women to political action. In this respect, survival concerns our biological life, standards of living, or ways of life.[30] Experiencing multiple jeopardy, or victimization based on many structural inequities, Black women adopt multiple identities—for example, Black, Afro-Caribbean, and woman—and demonstrate multiple levels of consciousness to bring about radical, profound and lasting social change.

In very similar ways to Black consciousness, the gender consciousness of Black women as "women" has been informed by resistance politics, including those of nationalist struggles and of the intercontinental women's movement. Kumari Jayawardena in her groundbreaking work, *Feminism and Nationalism in the Third World,* demonstrates through penetrating historical studies that women's consciousness is not a Western-inspired or foreign ideology in Third World or Southern countries (or, for that matter, in women-of-colour communities of Northern countries). She documents the inescapable fact that "women's movements do not occur in a vacuum but correspond to and, to some extent, are determined by the wider social movements of which they form part."[31] While Jayawardena's work looks at women in Asian societies, her theories have ample relevance to Black women in Asia and elsewhere.

In 1955, anti-apartheid resistance by South Africans, organized by oppressed "women," predated the onset of the modern women's movement by at least ten years. They refused to accept identification passes, which regulated the Blacks' mobility and which, until that time, had only been required of African men. When the racist minority regime attempted to extend pass laws to Black women and their children, two thousand Black women, singing hymns, converged on the capital, Pretoria, in a massive demonstration against government authorities. The women's pass campaign grew until it was nationwide, resulting in mass trials and imprisonment for hundreds of women.

Among activist Black women, it is generally recognized that nationalist struggle provides a rich arena for developing a woman's consciousness. Ounei recounts the effects of her discussions about the role of women in the Kanak independence movement with other women during their mutual political imprisonment. Upon release from prison, these women brought their concerns to the male leaders:

> It is not natural that you should speak in the plaza to thousands of people about doing away with the exploitation of man by man, while...you exploit your wives. You sit in a comfortable chair while the women do everything.[32]

Ounei recollects how criticisms about the treatment of women were not well-received by the men in the movement: "At that time, the men wanted to talk about Kanak independence and the unconditional return of Kanak land, but they didn't want to deal with the status of Kanak women. They accused us of being too theoretical."[33] However, under pressure, the different independence parties established women's sections. In 1982, the women founded the Group of Kanak and Exploited Women and eventually played a role in the movement's Central Committee. Of their political objectives and response to intergroup violence against Kanak women, Ounei says women "work inside the liberation movement to change the exploitative attitude men hold toward women. At the same time we work against colonialism, recognizing that it was colonialism that deformed the minds of our grandfathers. We women are the only ones who address the problems of battered and raped women and of teenage pregnancies."[34]

Like Ounei, Eva Johnson of Australia also believes that a correlation exists between women's oppression and the colonial experience. She indicts colonialism for the introduction of alcohol and the attendant abuse of Aboriginal women and girls by battering, rape, and incest: "Incest is nontraditional in that it was never practised in Aboriginal tradition in Australia. I see it as a white habit."[35] From Johnson's perspective, "Black men are adopting all forms of white values and strategies to fight against Black women or to use as their power against Black women. All of these are very important to address."[36]

Commonplace crimes against women prevail in India too. The Aryan (Hindu) culture's patriarchal gods supplanted the Dalit matriarchal system, instituting the devaluation of women with practices such as sati, or widow-burning.[37] The impact of the upper caste men's attitudes on Dalit women has been particularly devastating. According to Prema Shanta Kumari, a Dalit woman, "From time immemorial, the patriarchal society considered women as chattel, devoid of the freedom to belong to herself...especially in the Dalit community...The net result was that they were uneducated, illiterate, and kept in ignorance."[38] To reverse Dalit women's socio-economic condition of malnutrition, unsanitary conditions, hunger, unemployment, and indebtedness, activists advocate grassroots organizing, village by village, to "discuss their...problems, community issues and local atrocities committed on the basis of caste and sex."[39]

In much the same manner as the Dalit women activists view the situation, Germany's Black women activists insist that consciousness raising is fundamental for transformation. By Oguntoye's account, "feminists and lesbians are visible and alive in the Initiative of Black Germans...[and they] try to break the traditional role of man and woman that says men do the politics and women do the cooking and child care."[40] It is important, however, that the gender conflict is not allowed to separate Black Germans, given their relatively small population and the absence of Black neighbourhoods:

> We try to accept each other as lesbians, feminists, heterosexual women and men, and political and nonpolitical persons. Everyone should be able to be in the group and feel comfortable. I admit that it is not easy but we try as we cannot

really afford to be separated from each other. Who would have an advantage out of our separation anyway? For sure, not we the Black people in Germany.[41]

Certainly, the women's movement and the United Nations Decade for Women (1976-1985) have contributed to and augmented the gender consciousness that nationalist struggles have inspired in Black women.

The intercontinental dimensions of women's solidarity, as well as important international women's forums for dialogue and analysis, have served to strengthen Black women's advocacy on behalf of their own survival and that of the less powerful, including children, the elderly, and the sick. In many cases, we have formed our own organizations, demanding social and political participation, fairness in the allocation of economic resources, and reinterpretations of our cultures. In some cases, emphasis is on consciousness-raising within mixed-gender communities and organizations. In most instances, Black women seek empowerment through both types of political organizing: as members of their cultural groups, and as women.

The Black consciousness and women's movements have, no doubt, had an enduring impact on Black women's identity. In the International Cross-Cultural Black Women's Studies Summer Institute, we accept the array of definitions of Black identity because of our intercontinental nature, embracing various histories, struggles, and priorities of Black women to achieve humanhood and wholeness. The same principle applies to the diversity in women's consciousness. An integral aspect of our political movement entails learning from our commonalities and our differences. As such, the Institute's continued growth and development require respecting our cultural diversity and the struggles of our respective foremothers.

With all our diversity, we are bound by a common commitment to a qualitatively enhanced future for the living and the unborn. For we recognize that, as Black women, we are disproportionate victims of the world economic order, environmental degradation, disease, and narcotics. We are evidence that the intercontinental Black women's consciousness movement realizes that our individual and collective strength mandates crossing borders of many types, connecting, and nurturing our bonds to each other—whether we be indigenous women, Southern women, Northern women, racially oppressed women, ethnic minority women, immigrant women, migrant-worker women, rural women, refugee women, or women of different ages, with varied personal histories, and belonging to diverse religious faiths, political ideologies, social classes and cultures.

1 McLaughlin, A.N. (1989), 150.
2 Gaidzanwa, R. (1988), 6.
3 Nava, B.B. (1985), 7.
4 Ibid., 7.
5 Ibid., 7.
6 Ibid., 7.
7 Gaidzanwa, 6.
8 Johnson, E. (1989), 10.
9 Ibid., 10.
10 Ibid., 10.
11 Ibid., 10.
12 Ibid., 11.
13 Ibid., 11.
14 Oguntoye, K. (1988), 1.
15 Ibid., 2
16 Ibid., 2.
17 Ibid., 3.
18 Ibid., 3.
19 See McLaughlin (1989) for a comprehensive discussion of Black women's identity in South Africa, Aotearoa, Great Britain, and the United States.
20 Ibid., 159, n.21.
21 Ibid., 163, n.31.
22 Ibid., 163, n.34.
23 Ibid., 164, n.37.
24 Rajshekar, V. T. (1987), 40, 43.
25 McLaughlin (1989), 154, n.5.
26 Khanga, Y. (1989), 60.
27 Adade, C. Q. (1993), 2.
28 McLaughlin (1989), 167, n.45.
29 See McLaughlin for an analysis of the relationship among culture, social class, and political class, p. 155, n.7.
30 McLaughlin (1989), 174.
31 Jayawardena, K. (1986), 10.
32 Nava (1985), 7.
33 Ibid., 7, 8.
34 Ibid., 8.
35 Johnson (1989), 12.
36 Ibid., 12.
37 Rajshekar (1987), 43, 44.
38 Shantha, P. K. (1991), 16.
39 Ibid., 17.
40 Oguntoye (1988), 3.
41 Ibid., 4.

Bibliography

Adade, Charles Quist. (1993, March 27). "African-Russians Cry Out: 'We're an Endangered Species,' " *The New York Amsterdam News*, New York.

Afigbo, A. (1967). "Revolution and Reaction in East Nigeria 1900-1920," *Journal of the Historical Society of Nigeria*, Vol. III, No. 3, pp. 539-557.

Amadiume, Ifi. (1987). *Male Daughters and Female Husbands*. London: Zed Press.

Andaiye. (1994). "The Valuing of Women's Unwaged Work." Barbados: WAND.

Antrobus, Peggy. (1994). "The Community of Rosehall: a Model of Sustainable Human Development." Barbados: WAND.

Antrobus, Peggy. (1989). "Gender Implications of the Debt Crisis," in George Beckford & Norman Girvan (Ed.) *Development in Suspense*, Kingston. Friedrich Ebert Stiftung.

Bishop, Maurice. (1984). "For the cultural sovereignty of the Caribbean people," an address at the opening of the Caribbean Conference of Intellectual Workers, St. Georges Grenada, 20th November, 1982 in Chris Searle (Ed.) *In Nobody's Backyard;* Maurice Bishop's speeches 1979-1983, a memorial volume. London: Zed Books.

Clarke, George Elliott (Ed.). (1991). *Fire on the Water. An Anthology of Black Nova Scotian Writing*. Volume One. Nova Scotia: Pattersfield Press.

Davis, Angela. (1984). *Women, Culture, & Politics*. New York: Random House.

Davis, Angela. (1981). *Women, Race and Class*. New York: Random House.

Deere, Carmen Diana, et al. (1990). *In the Shadow of the Sun: Caribbean Development Alternatives and U.S.Policy.* Boulder: Westview Press..

Douglass, Frederick. (1982; first pub.1845). *Narrative of the Life of Frederick Douglass, an American Slave.* Harmondsworth, England; and New York: Penguin Books.

Ellis, Patricia. (1983). "The Rosehall Experience—Bottom-up Planning," in Planning for *Women in Rural Development. A Source Book for the Caribbean.* Barbados: WAND.

Elwert, George. (1984). "Conflicts Inside and Outside the Household: A West Africa Case Study" in Joan Smith, I. Wallerstein and Hans-Dieter Evers (Eds.).

Ekejiuba, Felicia. (1992). "Omu Okwei, the Merchant Queen of Osomari" in Bolanle Awe (Ed.) *Nigerian Women in Historical Perspectives.* Lagos: Sankore.

Ekejiuba, Felicia. (1984). "Contemporary Households and Major Socio-economic Transitions in E. Nigeria" in Jane Guyer and Pauline Peters (Eds.).

Elder, J.D. (1988). *African Survivals in Trinidad and Tobago.* London: Karla Press.

Fanon, Frantz. (1967). *The Wretched of the Earth.* Harmondsworth: Penguin.

Fanon, Frantz. (1967). *Black Skin, White Masks.* Translated by Charles Lam Markmann. New York: Grove Press.

Gaidzanwa, Rudo. (1988, Winter). "Feminism: The Struggle Within The Struggle," *Network: A Pan-African Women's Forum,* Harare, Zimbabwe, 1, no. 1.

Geerhart, J.D. (1986). "Farming Systems Research, Productivity, and Equity" in Moock, J.L. (Ed.).

Gutzmore, Cecil. (1986). *Caribbean Woman: Many Labours and Many Struggles. An Exhibition of Historical and Contemporary Images of Caribbean Women.* London: University of London.

Guyer, Jane. (1986). "Intra-household and Farming Systems Research: Perspectives from Anthropology" in Moock Joyce (Ed.).

Guyer, J. (Ed.) (1984). *Reconceptualising the Household: Issues of Theory, Method and Application.* Workshop Proceedings on "Reconceptualising the Household" held at the Harvard Institute of International Development, Cambridge, Massachusetts.

Guyer, Jane and Peters, Pauline. (1986). "Conceptualizing the Household: Issues of Theory and Policy in Africa," *Development and Change,* 18 (2), p. 197-214.

Hart, Richard. (1985). *Slaves who Abolished Slavery.* Kingston: University of West Indies.

Herskovits, Melville. (1947). *Trinidad Village.* New York: Octagon Press.

Hill, Polly. (1967). *Rural Hausa,* Oxford University Press, UK.

Jayawardena, Kumari. (1986). *Feminism and Nationalism in The Third World.* London: Zed Books.

Jewell, Terry L. (Ed.) (1993). *The Black Woman's Gumbo Ya-Ya. Quotations by Black Women.* Freedom, California: The Crossing Press.

Johnson, Eva. (1989, 5-11 March). "Claiming My Mothers, Exposing Aboriginal Consciousness to the World." Interview with Aboriginal, Black lesbian playwright Eva Johnson, Gay Community News, Boston, 16, no. 33.

Jones, C.W. (1986). "Intra-household Bargaining in Response to the Introduction of New Crops: A Case Study from N. Cameroons" in Joyce Moock (Ed.), *Understanding Africa's Rural Household.*

Khanga, Yelena. (1989, August). "Black Russian," *Essence Magazine,* New York, 20, n. 4. See also Yelena Khanga's *Soul to Soul: The Story of A Black Russian American Family, 1865-1992,* W.W. Norton & Co., New York, 1992.

Lamming, George. *The Role of the Intellectual in the Caribbean.* Cimarron, 1 (1), 13-18.

Mathurin, Lucille. (1975). "The Arrivals of Black Women." *Jamaica Journal,* 9 (2 and 3), 2-7.

Mathurin, Lucille. (1975). *The Rebel Woman in the British West Indies During Slavery.* Jamaica: The Afro-Caribbean Institute of Jamaica.

Mba, N. (1980). *Nigerian Women Mobilized.* University of California Press.

McLaughlin, Andrée Nicola. (1989). "Black Women, Identity, and the Quest for Humanhood and Wholeness: Wild Women in the Whirlwind," in Joann Braxton and Andrée Nicola McLaughlin (Eds.), *Wild Women in the Whirlwind: Afra-American Culture and The Contemporary Literary Renaissance,* Rutgers University Press, New Brunswick, N.J.

Memmi, Albert. (1990). *The Colonizer and the Colonized.* Translated by Howard Greenfield; Introduction by Jean-Paul Sartre; new introduction by Liam O'Dowd. London: Earthscan.

Momsen, Janet. (1993). *Women and Change in the Caribbean.* Bloomington: Indiana University Press.

Moock, Joyce L. (Ed.) (1986). *Understanding Africa's Rural Households and Farming Systems.* Boulder: Westview Press.

Nava, Beatrice B. (1985, December). "New Caledonia Women Participate in The Struggle for Independence: A WIRE Interview with Susanna Ounei," *Women's International Resource Exchange (WIRE)*, New York.

Nettleford, Rex. (1970). *Mirror, Mirror. Identity, Race and Protest in Jamaica.* Jamaica: Collins and Sangster.

Oguntoye, Katharina. (1988, 19 July). "Naming Our Condition: The Afro-German Movement," an unpublished paper presented at The International Cross-Cultural Black Women's Studies Summer Institute, New York.

Okonjo, K. (1976). "Rotating Credit Unions Among Midwestern Igbo Women," *Studies in Family Planning*, Special Issue on Learning About Rural Women, The Population Council, New York.

Osei, G.K. (1979). *Caribbean Women, Their History and Habits.* London: African Publication Society.

Pala, Okeyo. (1980). "Daughters of the Lakes and Rivers: Colonization and the Land Rights of Luo Women" in Mona Etienne and Eleanor Leacock (Eds.). *Women and Colonization: Anthropological Perspectives.* J.F. Bergin Publishers.

Patterson, Orlando. (1967). *The Sociology of Slavery.* London: McGibbon and Kee.

Peters, Pauline. (1986). "Household Management in Botswana: Cattle, Crops and Wage Labor" in Moock J. L. (Ed.).

Rajshekar, V.T. (1987). *Dalit: The Black Untouchables of India.* Ottawa: Clarity Press.

Rodney, Walter. (1981). *The History of the Guyanese Working People: 1881-1905.* London: Heinemann Educational Publications.

Rodney, Walter. (1969, October). "Guinea and the Significance of the Origins of Africans Enslaved in the New World." *Journal of Negro History*, LIV, 327-345.

Rogers, Barbara. (1980). *The Domestication of Women.* New York: Tavistock Publications.

Shantha, Prema Kumari. (1991). "The Role of Women in the Christian Dalit Liberation Movement," in Jean Sindab (Ed.), *Women Under Racism: A Decade of Visible Action, World Council of Churches*, Programme to Combat Racism, Geneva.

Silverblatt, I. (1987). *Moon, Sun and Witches: Gender Ideologies and Class in Inca and Colonial Peru*, Princeton University Press, New Jersey.

Simms, Glenda. (1990). "Racism and Sexism in the 90s," Florence Bird Lecture, Carleton University.

Smith, Joan, Immanuel Wallerstein, and Hans-Dieter Evers. (1984). *Households, and the World Economy*. California: Sage.

Springer, Eintou Pearl. (1992, March). "Women Yesterday, Today; Contributory Factors to the Plight of Today's Afro-Caribbean Woman." Paper delivered on International Women's Day, St. Vincent Projects Promotions, Kingstown. Pamphlet.

Springer, Eintou Pearl. (1991). *Focussed*. Oxford: Oxford Triangle Press.

Springer, Eintou Pearl. (1990, August). "The Caribbean Woman, Burden Bearer of the Race." *African Commentary*.

Springer, Eintou Pearl. (1984). "The Role of Culture in Emancipation." Paper delivered at the Commemoration of 150 years of Human Development, St. Johns, Antigua. Unpublished.

Stauth, George. (1984). "Households, Modes of Living and Production Systems" in Joan Smith, I. Wallerstein and H. Evers (Ed.).

Sunshine, Catherine. (1985). *The Caribbean: Survival, Struggle and Sovereignty*. EPICA Publication.

Van Sertima, Ivan. (1976). *They Came Before Columbus*. New York: Random House.

Walker, Alice. (1982). *The Color Purple*. New York: Simon and Schuster.

Warner-Lewis, M. (1990). *Guinea's Other Suns*. Massachusetts: Majority Press.

Washington, Mary Helen. (1991). *Invented Lives: Narratives of Black Women, 1860-1960*. New York: Doubleday.

Wolf, Naomi. (1990). *The Beauty Myth*. Toronto: Random House.

Wong, D. (1984). "The Limits of Using the Household as a Unit of Analysis" in Joan Smith, et al (Eds.).

Wright Phillip (Ed.). (Rev. 1966; First pub. 1907). *Lady Nugent's Journal of Her Residence in Jamaica from 1801 to 1805*. Kingston: Institute of Jamaica.

Wright, Richard. (1942). *Native Son*. New York: Modern Library.

Young, Carlene. (Ed.). (1972). *Black Experience, Analysis and Synthesis*. California: Leswing Press.